# Teaching and Training Techniques for Hospital Doctors

*Edited by*

Trevor Bayley

and

Michael Drury

RADCLIFFE MEDICAL PRESS

© 1998 Trevor Bayley and Michael Drury

Radcliffe Medical Press Ltd
18 Marcham Road, Abingdon, Oxon OX14 1AA

British Library Cataloguing in Publication Data

A catalogue record for this book is available from the British Library.

ISBN 1 85775 173 6

Typeset by Acorn Bookwork, Salisbury, Wiltshire
Printed and bound by Biddles Ltd, Guildford and King's Lynn

# Contents

# Preface

*'...teaching skills are not necessarily innate but can be learned...'*
GMC Education Committee's Recommendations on the Training of
Specialists (1987).

The idea for this book was the discussion on teaching doctors how to
teach in meetings of the Standing Committee on Postgraduate Medical
and Dental Education (SCOPME) of which the editors have been
members. Although training the trainers, as part of vocational training for
general medical practice in the UK, has been one of the outstanding
educational successes of the National Health Service, the same cannot be
said of the acquisition of teaching and learning skills in other branches of
the profession, particularly in hospital-based specialties. Since the reforms
to specialist medical training, recommended by the Chief Medical
Officer's Working Group in 1993, many hospital consultants have
acknowledged that, whatever the etymology of the title, doctor, there was
a need for most to learn teaching and training skills.

This book is intended to provide, in a readable form, insight to the
methods and skills needed to be a better trainer. Whilst some may wish to
attend one of the growing number of courses offered by a variety of
providers, this book is an alternative for those who prefer to read to learn.
It is also complementary to a course.

The authors of the chapters have been or are actively involved in
postgraduate medical education. Some are hospital doctors, others are
eminent general practitioners with many years experience in teaching
others to teach. The theory of education and training has not been
covered in any of the chapters, which have been written with the aim of
practical use of the training and assessment methods described.

Trevor Bayley
Michael Drury
*August 1998*

# List of contributors

Dr Trevor Bayley
Postgraduate Dean
Postgraduate Education and
  Training Department
Hamilton House
24 Pall Mall
Liverpool   L3 6AL


Mr Stephen Brearley
Consultant Surgeon and Surgical
  Tutor
Whipps Cross Hospital
Whipps Cross Road
Leytonstone
London   E11


Mr Joseph Campbell
Department of Postgraduate
  Studies
University of Wales College of
  Medicine
Heath Park
Cardiff   CF4 4XN

Dr Tim Dornan
Hospital Dean for Clinical Studies
Hope Hospital
Stott Lane
Salford
Manchester   M6 8HD

Professor Tom Hayes
Postgraduate Dean
Department of Postgraduate
  Studies
University of Wales College of
  Medicine
Heath Park
Cardiff   CF4 4XN

Emeritus Professor David Metcalfe
Westgate Barn
Milburn
Penrith
Cumbria   CA10 1TW

Professor Carl Whitehouse
Department of General Practice
Rusholme Health Centre
Walmer Street
Manchester   M14 5NP

# Acknowledgements

The editors thank the contributors for their willingness to write according to a brief, Radcliffe Medical Press for its patience and Angela McMahon, Mersey Deanery, for her cheerful tolerance in undertaking additional work from one of the editors.

# Introduction

*'The quality of care which the NHS can deliver rests entirely on the high standards and excellence of the training, education, and teaching which it provides.'*

The words not of a medical educator but of a politician, the then Secretary of State for Health, Kenneth Clarke; a sentiment which he repeated when outlining the ten key principles for the arrangements for delivery of postgraduate medical and dental education, following the NHS reforms in 1990.

Further emphasis on the importance of teaching for hospital specialists has followed the reforms in specialist medical training, introduced after the Chief Medical Officer's Working Group report *Hospital Doctors: Training for the Future*. Shorter, more structured training, with progress based on competence, would it was recognized, require more intensive tuition. The Standing Committee on Postgraduate Medical and Dental Education, SCOPME, recognized the importance of improving the learning environment in hospitals through improving the teaching skills of consultants. Several of the medical royal colleges have also identified the need to provide 'teaching for teachers' courses. Slowly, a cadre of doctors who have learned how to teach, supervise, and appraise has increased – but many remain whose teaching 'skills' are based on their own experiences as undergraduates or doctors in training.

'Teaching skills are not innate', as recognized by the Education Committee of the General Medical Council, yet all doctors in independent practice are expected to accept 'responsibility for training junior colleagues ... and teaching other doctors, medical students, and other health care professionals'. The skills that some teachers employ are those used by their own teachers, often described as 'teaching (or learning) by humiliation'. The same is untrue for teaching and learning in general medical practice: in that 'specialty' teachers must learn how to teach, must be approved and reapproved as trainers, and must demonstrate that they are maintaining those skills. The example of general medical practice has been slowly adopted by those responsible for training in other specialties.

Teaching is more than transfer of knowledge. The model adopted by GP educators, the so-called educational triangle of aims, methods, and assessment, is equally applicable to other specialties and other health professions.

The aim of any teaching programme has to be defined to help the learner understand the educational objectives, to assist the teacher, and to clarify the relationship between the teacher and learner.

The methods used for teaching and learning also require clear definition at the outset. What equipment and resources, not necessarily financial, are needed? In this way the most appropriate method will be selected, be it attendance at a course, taking part in small-group discussion, one-to-one teaching, or any other. GP educators make use of formal recording of some teaching sessions, both to enhance learning and to elaborate on what has been taught. Recording could be used more frequently in other specialties, particularly to analyse suitability of teaching techniques.

All teaching should be subject to assessment of the learning achieved by the individual or the group (e.g. evaluation of a course). Many still regard assessment as meaning examinations; and such a perception leads to the dominance of assessment over learning. Assessment should aid and support both teacher and learner, and encourage comparison between learners and the teaching methods, with the objective of improvement.

It is not the purpose of this book to provide a description of learning theories. Broadly, theories of learning are either 'simple' or 'developed'. 'Simple' theories depend on the belief that if a topic has been taught it must have been learnt. At the core of such theories is the precept that the teacher has full control over the process and the result. This 'teacher-centred' approach is common in postgraduate medical education.

'Developed' theories of learning see the learner as a partner, contributing to the learning experience. The teacher uses accumulated experience and expertise to facilitate learning, to help the learner to identify educational needs, and to relate what is to be learned to personal experience.

From an understanding of learning theory follows various approaches to, or theories of, teaching. The most common approach is what might be called transfer theory: knowledge is regarded as an article which can be transferred. To facilitate transmission of information, facts are presented in a more easily understood form. The process of transfer is based on the 'simple' theory of learning: teaching of the topic, it is assumed, must be followed by gaining of knowledge. The teacher has taught and thus the learner must have learned! This emphasis on facts is redolent of the attitude towards teaching and learning of the character Thomas Gradgrind, created by Charles Dickens in his novel *Hard Times*. Dickens satirizes the setting up of teacher-training programmes in 1846, with the aim of improving universal education, as developing memory at the expense of intelligence.

Teaching may be considered as a process of 'shaping' the learner's intellect. The teacher seeks to produce and develop connections in the student's mind through lectures and demonstrations. This approach also contains the Gradgrind 'philosophy of fact': its aim is only part understanding, part indoctrination.

A more learner-centred approach to teaching is that based on the 'travelling theory' of teaching. The teacher seeks to guide, lead, and point the direction of learning. This theory treats education as an odyssey: a lifelong eventful journey with hills, mountains, and plains. The pace of learning during this journey varies; and the teacher must take account of this.

The mind changes and grows with time. Another theory of teaching is that of cultivation of the intellect. The teacher seeks to influence growth of knowledge, skills, and attitudes during the learning process. The 'growing' theory of teaching is probably the most learner-centred approach: seeking to identify and assess the learning needs of the individual; how these relate to existing knowledge, skills, and attitudes; and their relevance to the professional task.

The purpose of this book is to provide a practical guide for hospital doctors wishing to become better teachers. The intended readership is not educationists, rather the practising doctor who perceives a need to enhance his or her teaching skills in the wards, out-patient clinic, and theatre. It is also intended to help those who have responsibility for planning teaching programmes and who need to select appropriate teaching methods. Improvement in teaching also depends on assessment of those who have been taught and evaluation of teaching programmes.

If the reader uses the text to plan teaching, whether of knowledge, skills, or attitudes, and subsequently evaluates that through feedback provided by assessment, it will have been successful. If it encourages the reflective teacher, it will be more so.

# 1 Learning principles

*Trevor Bayley*

Choosing the best strategy for teaching, whether it be in a clinic or on a ward round, in an operating theatre or in a tutorial group, requires an understanding of some of the principles of how postgraduate 'students' learn. Although such principles are not based on an exact science, experience shows that adults learn best under certain conditions:

- when what is to be learned is relevant to their practice
- when learning is related to their previous experience
- when the learner is helped to recognize self-learning needs
- when the learner is involved in planning learning
- when the learner evaluates the learning experience.

Adoption of these principles gives teaching and learning a developmental aspect rather than simply transmission of facts. Using these principles learning will probably be faster, and what has been learned retained longer.

## Motivation to learn

It is a self-evident truth that the learner who wants to learn probably does so faster – and in greater depth. The motivation for learning is sometimes an examination or other assessment; on other occasions it may be the topic is of interest. Selection of what is learned is particularly obvious among adult learners, who are most concerned to acquire knowledge and skills relevant to their everyday work and practice. Such selection may not be compatible with attempts to broaden learning. Learners may repeatedly select a topic of interest rather than seek new knowledge and skills which may be valuable in their practice at some stage in the future.

Hence the importance of setting learning objectives which take account of previous experience and identify lack of knowledge and skills that are or will be needed.

Examinations and assessments often enhance the motivation to learn. Anxiety and tension about the outcome of these may not encourage deep learning and understanding; rather superficial learning, of brief duration, which lacks true understanding (often because what is 'learned' has little relevance to clinical practice and everyday work).

Motivation may be enhanced by offering rewards. Such a tactic may not always achieve learning with understanding. Again, learning for reward may not be wholly successful if the learner has not played a part in identifying the learning need. Clearly, learning is not facilitated and the learner is not motivated if the teacher adopts an aggressive or punitive approach, seeking to correct rather than encouraging an open discussion.

## The learning environment or 'climate'

The relationship between learner and teacher is self-evidently a major factor in the educational process. If both teacher and learner enjoy the wish for greater knowledge and enhanced skills, a better learning environment is created. Adult learners respond to teaching if they perceive their ability and needs are respected. A 'partnership' between teacher and learner is, for many, an enabling relationship, facilitating self-assessment and planning of further education and training. Both parties may find this a difficult relationship; some teachers, in particular, prefer to regard the relationship as a gradient between the teacher, with greater knowledge and skills, and the learner who receives these by a process of diffusion. Such a relationship is rarely enabling and does not centre the teaching process on the learner.

Learners must be able to ask questions without fear of humiliation. Unfortunately, much medical teaching in the past was based on humiliation, often to the amusement of those watching and listening. Such attitudes are unlikely if the teacher and learner work together to solve problems, in a partnership. Both teacher and learner gain from this: not only do both learn but mutual respect, which facilitates education and training, develops.

The location of teaching can either encourage or detract from learning. For 'mass' education the lecture theatre is suitable; however, the value of the formal lecture as anything more than a least costly means of transmission of information is doubted by most teachers. More effective is the small group, usually in a tutorial room with suitable seating and appropriate audio-visual aids. Small-group learning has the advantage that chairs can be arranged so that participants see each other – not each other's backs. A circular arrangement of members of a small group encourages discussion; and the teacher – or resource as the teacher may be called – as part of that circle is not separate from learners, behind a desk or on a dais. Distractions are fewer in small groups than in a lecture, or when the teacher is before the 'class', behind a desk. Individual appraisal or teaching is best conducted with an informal seating arrangement, not with teacher and trainee on opposite sides of a desk.

The learning environment is easily disturbed by a 'bleeping' pager or telephone call. Such 'damage to the climate' should be limited by ensuring that time for teaching is protected from any interference. To achieve this it may be necessary to repeat the tutorial or teaching session; one half of the learners attending the session whilst the other is involved in the service.

## Speech and action

Actual delivery of teaching can influence its effectiveness. Short, clear sentences are much easier for the learner to comprehend. Too often teaching is delivered as short but unfinished sentences. The addition of qualifying clauses can disturb the flow of words, again having adverse effect on understanding because of loss of clarity. Meaning may be lost, for the listener, if a teacher seeks to qualify too often during a session. On the other hand, if a new technical term is introduced it is best to stop and ask whether anyone has any knowledge of this, explaining if necessary, and continuing once there is understanding.

Diagrams are an important aid to learning, possibly used too infrequently by most teachers. The combination of visual and verbal messages is particularly helpful in teaching a practical skill. It is difficult to explain a practical skill in words; it is much easier with a simple sketch, however crude. This is a valuable aid whether during a lecture, in a small group, or one-to-one teaching. It is helpful to involve the trainee in drawing the diagram.

## Subject relevance

As already mentioned, an important principle of adult learning is that the learner perceives the subject matter of a teaching session to be relevant to both present and future clinical practice. In this way, learning is probably deeper and quicker. The adult learner is usually well aware of learning needs, sometimes through audit, and also knows what is relevant to his/her practice.

Previous experience is also important to learning: it is easier to build on previous knowledge, experience, and skills, creating links between these and what is yet to be learned. In drawing up a learning plan it is important to identify the previously acquired skills and knowledge. Repetition of previous skills teaching can be avoided if plans are based on the practical record or log book of the learner. For this reason, among others, all doctors in training should be encouraged to keep a record of experience, either in the form of a journal or log.

## Learning by doing

Learning is an active process which uses recall of information previously acquired as well as that being taught. Many learners find they learn best by doing, either whilst carrying out the procedure, or afterwards on reflection, or a combination of both. Supervision is an important element of such learning: it may be provided at different levels, from direct oversight of the conduct of a procedure to availability of the supervisor to be recalled as needed. Level of supervision is particularly important in some specialties, such as anaesthetics. The novice clearly requires immediate supervision; the more experienced learner needs to be allowed some freedom from direct oversight, although assistance has always to be available.

Simulation can be a useful early learning process, the learner 'going live' when confidence has been acquired using an appropriate model. Many surgical procedures are particularly amenable to simulation, for example fashioning a bowel or vascular anastomosis or preforming a surgical procedure through a fibreoptic instrument. Use of endoscopic instruments is also a skill that can be taught initially using simulation.

Simulation is also useful in formative and summative assessment. In the same way that it is possible to assess the skills of airline pilots in simulated situations, simulation can be used to assess skills such as the management of trauma and cardiopulmonary resuscitation.

## Discussion teaching

Discussion teaching is a form of active learning; it involves a two-way discussion of subjects between teacher and learners. Discussion teaching requires confidence between members of the group and an understanding that contributions are made 'in private', thus encouraging free debate without any member fearing humiliation. The teacher, too, learns by this process but he or she can feel threatened.

Free expression and prompt feedback are important features of the learning process of discussion teaching: these allow assessment of what has been learned and the opportunity to correct errors in understanding and ideas. Unlike many small-group learning groups, it is important that all members of the group take part in the debate. The teacher, as chairman, must ensure that each member contributes to the discussion: hence the need for confidence between the group. Unless each member joins the debate it is not possible to know what has been learned and what misunderstanding there may have been.

Discussion is considered by its proponents to be a powerful form of teaching. It requires experienced teachers who are able to manage open debate – those who can also build confidence in the most diffident learner.

## Role playing

Like simulation of technical procedures, role playing can achieve 'virtual reality'. It is, for most, an enjoyable way of learning; and it is enduring. Carefully planned, even scripted, role play is a means of simulating situations which occur in real life – thus preparing the learner to deal with these when they occur. The learner is prepared for the situation and should both perform better and gain more from the 'real thing'.

The learning power of role play can be enhanced by video- and audio-taping; by replaying the tape it is possible to identify those things which have been well done as well as those aspects that require improvement. Video-taping a patient consultation can be a valuable means of assessment in general practice training. Similarly, it is of value in the training of psychiatrists, for example in the conduct of family therapy. In both cases simulated patients may be used: actors who have learned the role of a patient or family member. In North America, in particular, professional patient simulators have an important role both in teaching and assessment.

Role play is also useful in improving communication and presentation skills. Peer review of a presentation plus a video recording is a useful means of helping a learner prepare to speak at a scientific or public meeting.

## Feedback

Most learners complain that they rarely receive feedback on their performance. Advice on what was well done – and what was not – can be useful both in learning a technical procedure and other skills. If feedback is given by an experienced teacher it can be of educational value, enabling the learner to identify learning needs and to plan strategies for learning by encouraging reflection. Formative assessment, if it is to be learner-centred and effective, should include feedback.

Feedback should never be censorious if it is to be educationally valuable. It is not helpful, therefore, to begin feedback with critical comment. However poor the performance, it is best to begin by discussing those aspects which were well done, even if few.

Feedback is also a feature of problem-based learning: the learner is provided with information which helps with the solution of a clinical problem. Decision-making skills can also be facilitated by feedback, as part of role play. The decision-maker is provided with information on the effects of his/her action, had this been 'real life'.

## Evidence-based problem solving

The process of making decisions on the basis of known evidence is a variation of problem solving and, it is claimed, achieves greater retention of learning than many other methods. Evidence, including history, examination, and investigation, plus research, is applied to decision making. Gaps in knowledge and uncertainties are filled by research evidence which has been critically appraised. The assessed evidence is not, however, a substitute for clinical skills nor experience, but is used to enhance decision making.

Ward rounds, meetings, and small-group discussions can all be a means for using evidence-based medicine. For example, on a ward round doctors are asked to give reasoned arguments for clinical decisions. First the evidence of the history and examinations is considered, and the inferences that should be drawn from these discussed. The evidence from investigations is then considered and again inferences are made. Clinical and investigational evidence is then enhanced by the use of critically appraised literature both in making the diagnosis and making decisions on clinical management. The ward round is used to identify questions that should be answered by critical appraisal.

It is claimed that systematic application of research evidence and epidemiology enhances the motivation of doctors and students. Used by a firm or team, evidence-based medicine encourages debate and should enlarge the knowledge base of everyone. Effectiveness of clinical decisions should also be enhanced; and they should be made speedily.

## Self-directed learning

Studying on one's own is the way in which most learners prepare for examinations. Such learning can, however, be superficial. Learning in pairs is preferred by others. The 'buddy' system of learning is now one favoured strategy for continuing education and development. A pair of learners can help each other identify learning needs and discover 'gaps' although, clearly, there must be confidence between them.

Programmed learning is another example of self-directed learning. The learner proceeds by short steps, moving from one to the next when his/her ability to do so has been confirmed by 'passing a test' in the form of a problem. The process is time-consuming for the teacher. The learner can only progress, however, after achieving mastery. Learning is usually deep using such programmes, although it may not be sustained.

Many learn by performing 'project work'. The project may consist of reviewing a journal for a meeting, preparing a paper for presentation, or presentation at hospital 'grand rounds'. Searching for information may enhance learning, although this may not be sustained if the project lacks relevance to clinical experience and practice. Project work may also be used as part of summative assessment, notably by those specialties which require written presentation skills.

Keeping a logbook or journal may also help self-directed learning. The record of tasks completed and meetings/educational activities attended is useful to learner and teacher in planning future learning to fill 'gaps'. Log books and journals do not, however, indicate whether a task or procedure was done well although, for surgical procedures, a list of 'complications' resulting from the procedure may give some evidence of competence and performance.

### Key points

- Examinations and assessments may enhance learning but such learning is often superficial.
- The location of teaching can enhance or hinder learning.

- The learning environment is easily disturbed by bleeping pagers and telephone calls.

- Short sentences are easier for a learner to comprehend.

- New technical terms used in teaching should always be described when they are first introduced.

- Teaching is more effective if it builds on previous knowledge.

- Discussion teaching, involving two-way debate about topics between teacher and student, is a powerful means of teaching but requires confidence on both sides.

- Planned role play can achieve 'virtual reality' in preparing the learner for actual situations.

- The learning power of role play is enhanced by video-taping.

- Feedback should not be censorious if it is to be educationally valuable.

- Used by a clinical firm or team, evidence-based medicine encourages debate and should enlarge the knowledge base of all.

- Learning in pairs encourages identification of learning needs.

- Keeping of a log book encourages self-directed learning.

# 2 Teaching methods for consultants

## David Metcalfe

## Thinking about teaching: managing learning and setting objectives

The tradition that doctors teach their successors goes back to Hippocrates, and we quite often remind people that the very word 'Doctor' means 'Teacher'. Unfortunately, two factors have contributed to a general failure among clinicians to be as professional as teachers as they are as doctors: the need to maintain the 'mystery', and hence a tendency to keep things within the profession; and the imbalance of power between doctor and patient which washes over into a similar (and even more deleterious) relationship with those we are trying to teach, tomorrow's colleagues.

The best working definition of a teacher is that the 'teacher is the manager of learning'. (In a way this is analogous to the often forgotten fact that doctors do not heal, they provide the best conditions for the body to heal itself.) Given equal competence, the better doctor is the one who can put himself or herself in the patient's place when explaining the situation and discussing what to do – the doctor as teacher. Similarly, the good teacher should empathize with his or her learners. The fundamental consideration for those who teach, therefore, is not 'What should I teach?' but 'What should my pupils learn?'.

All theories of management agree on the need to set clear objectives, and managing learning is no exception: without them you cannot make rational choices on what to teach and how to teach it, nor can you assess whether the learners have got what you wanted them to get out of your teaching. Educational theory and practice (often derided as 'jargon' by doctors who fail to recognize that every profession has its shorthand and that if we want to profit from others' expertise we must learn their jargon) expects teachers to set objectives in three 'domains': knowledge, skills, and attitudes. This convention rests on the recognition that performance, which is after all what we want to improve by our teaching, rests not on knowledge alone but also on having the necessary skills, and having the appropriate attitudes. We all know colleagues who are very knowledgeable but ineffectual because they do not seem to be able to apply that knowledge or because they are unmotivated to do a good job.

The usefulness of such explicit objectives is that they allow the teacher to choose appropriate methods. The lecture is well suited to expanding understanding and can contribute a little to attitude formation, but nothing to skills, whether manual or intellectual. Manual skills have to be taught by the traditional cycle of demonstration, rehearsal under supervision, and feedback (even if using sophisticated equipment such as virtual reality). Intellectual skills of problem solving and decision making are the same and require the same cycle of learning. Attitudes are formed to some extent by role modelling, both positive ('I'd like to be like her…') and negative ('Whatever else, I hope I don't turn out to be like him…'), but much more by peer pressure. Accordingly, learning opportunities are needed which allow learners to express their feelings about people, situations, and tasks, and compare them to those of their peers. (Incidentally, this lets medical teachers off the hook of being open to accusations of 'brainwashing' or 'manipulation' which some fear or use as an excuse for avoiding the inculcation of appropriate attitudes.)

Setting such explicit objectives is unfamiliar and sometimes unpopular among medical teachers. For individual occasions it may be as effective to set less formal aims, in terms of 'What I want the learners to get out of this teaching is…', provided this is done sufficiently clearly to influence choice of both method and content. Perhaps the best way is to get into the habit of setting explicit objectives in the three domains before maturing into less formal routines in which the objectives are equally well thought out but implicit. It could be said that if you can't write down what your pupils will understand after your teaching that they didn't understand before, you shouldn't set out to teach them!

When designing a *course*, however, explicit objectives are essential for three reasons: they inform the choice of teachers and the way each one is briefed; they dictate the range of methods to be used and therefore the timetable and resources needed; and most importantly, they are essential to ensure the validity of any examination testing the learners' achievements.

**Key points**

- Know your learners.
- Consider what they need to learn from you.
- Set out your aims and objectives.
- Select what you need to put over.
- Choose the most effective way of doing it.

# Thinking about the learners

Those learning from us are as human as we are, and need to be considered as people whose feelings will affect their ability to take on board what we want them to learn. In designing our teaching we have to try to make it easy for them to learn. To do this we need to consider three things: who they are; how they feel; and what they need from us.

Who they are depends on where they are in their career in medicine: students will have different needs from colleagues at a postgraduate meeting or GPs on a refresher course. The first see learning as necessary to pass the next exam, the second to enhance their practice, the third to inform decisions about investigations, treatment, and referral. Those on courses, whether undergraduate or postgraduate, will want teaching that fits in with the rest: a teacher should make it his business to know what else has been taught and when. Remember that half of your learners will probably be women, and a sizeable proportion, though educated in the UK, will be from the ethnic minorities: both groups feel, and with reasons, that teachers often are insensitive to their sensitivities (for example, slipping in slides of partially clothed women unnecessarily 'to wake them up'). So the first duty of the teacher is to find out about his or her learners.

How they feel centres on their appreciation of where they stand in the power hierarchy. At a superficial level, for instance, proximity to exams will sharply focus their estimate of what is relevant and therefore acceptable. Below that there are layers and layers of feelings. Students feel very vulnerable. In a profession where knowing all about everything seems to be the minimum acceptable standard, they know how far short of that (illusory) ideal they fall. Their vulnerability makes them particularly sensitive to criticism, which if offered insensitively (as we all remember happening to us) they see as 'humiliation'. They have their dignity, and we do well to safeguard the dignity of all with less power than ourselves, whether patients or students. Doctors in the training grades are equally vulnerable, for we not only lead them and teach them but write their references! The fact that while we draw attention to their shortcomings, both publicly on rounds and privately in references, they cannot reciprocate about our feet of clay, of which they are well aware, warps the teacher–learner relationship. Lastly, remember that our traditional and very effective teaching strategy of getting learners to commit themselves ('Tell me if the spleen is enlarged...') and then giving them full and frank feedback is deeply uncomfortable for those from cultures where losing face is even more unacceptable than it is for the indigenous learners. So the second duty of the teacher is to devise learning opportunities which will minimize the power imbalance; when commitment is essential, feedback should be given in a way that respects and enhances the learner's dignity rather than damaging it.

What they need from us is not instruction, whether by precept or example, but help. As far as we have been able to we have mastered our part of the craft of medicine by putting together a huge variety of factual knowledge, incorporating a wide range of skills, developing attitudes to the job, our colleagues, and our patients, and learning to cope with uncertainty. Teaching aimed at transferring facts with which to satisfy some examiner is like teaching an animal to do tricks: humiliating to the learner and demeaning to the teacher! So the third duty of the teacher is to design his or her teaching to help the learner acquire competence.

---

**Key points**

- Consider the learners' career situations.
- Think about their feelings.
- Be aware of the imbalance of power.
- Think in terms of help rather than instruction.

---

# The main teaching methods and how to learn them

Clinicians use four main sorts of teaching method: the lecture, small-group teaching, ward rounds, and one-to-one tutorials. Each has its limitations and usefulness, and each demands skills which are learnable.

Teaching is like singing or playing an instrument: pretty well everybody can reach the level of making an acceptable contribution to a local choir or group, even if we cannot all be Pavarotti or Uchida, but we have to be prepared to learn from others, to practise, and to respond constructively to feedback (as, of course, do the great soloists). Teaching courses are useful, and widely available, but getting a colleague to sit in and provide feedback, getting learner feedback, and even video-recording your own teaching are desirable ways in which to enhance performance.

---

**Key points**

- Learners deserve professionalism from their teachers.
- Teaching is a learnable skill.
- Professionalism demands that teachers learn to teach.

---

## The lecture

The lecture is the most traditional teaching method in medical education. One of the reasons for this is its perceived 'efficiency' – one teacher can provide for a large number of learners. Any activity can only be 'efficient', however, if it is effective: if it does not achieve its objective it doesn't matter how parsimonious its use of resources has been. The lecture is not an effective way of transferring facts and the learning involved is passive: the listeners cannot use the knowledge they are being supplied with to explore its significance (and you are more likely to remember what you have used than what you have only tried to memorize).

The task of a lecturer is not to instruct but to explain; not to pontificate but to take the listeners on a journey of exploration. The purpose of a lecture is to share understanding: if you have been asked to lecture on a topic it is most likely because you have been seen to be an expert in the field, that is, someone who understands what is important, how it fits in with other knowledge, what its significance is, what remains unknown, and how to cope with uncertainty. (This is why lectures which begin by describing cases and what was done are well received: the speaker shows how all the expertise was applied, then 'dissects' it). Of course explaining something new to the learner requires an input of factual knowledge, but it also builds on previously held knowledge and should stimulate further acquisition of knowledge afterwards. (This is why knowing where your audience are in their careers is so important, and why using that well-worn postgraduate centre lecture and your favourite slides for an undergraduate session is unlikely to be effective. Just think of the differences in what you can expect the two audiences to know before you start! Furthermore, undergraduates want to take notes, unlike most postgraduates, which has implications for your pace as well as your choice of visual aids.

To give them some of your understanding you have to lead up to each crucial point with the necessary facts, and then crystallize it for your listeners. This should be reflected in the pace and volume of your presentation: let it have climaxes. You can review facts quite fast and at an even volume, but to hammer home your key point you can drop or raise your voice and slow down to emphasize that what they are getting now is the real nub of the thing. Don't be flat in either pace or volume.

To share understanding you need to:

- relate the matter to what your audience is likely to know already

- present new facts in terms of the way they contribute to understanding and connect up with each other ('So, because X, the result of Y is...')

- establish their relative importance ('Never forget that A...'; 'Most of the time B doesn't matter but when C it does')

- indicate their reliability, and correct common errors (including those in the textbooks)

- admit to what we don't yet know (thereby inculcating an ongoing interest).

Lectures can do two other things. Firstly they can indicate the limits to the learning required: what the audience does not need to bother with (perhaps until they enter your specialty at a senior level). Such indications are welcomed by undergraduates who, after the strictly defined curricula of A levels, find medicine worryingly open ended. Beware, however, of inculcating a closed curriculum mentality, the idea of a perimeter beyond which they do not need to learn, as opposed to the spine concept, where they must know the core but should adventure along the ribs too. The second thing a lecture can do is to influence attitudes (usually in a minatory way, warning off certain behaviours). This is done by describing real events, either successes or failures, and exposing your own feelings about what was done, thereby providing what might be called vicarious role modelling. Attitudes are changed only when emotions are engaged, and you will not engage your listeners' emotions unless you expose your own.

**Key points**

When asked to give a lecture you should:

- find out about your audience and, if your contribution is part of a course, what else has been taught in it

- consider their needs of understanding in the topic: their needs are your objectives

- prepare the lecture in the light of the above considerations (rather than getting the old favourite down off the shelf yet again!)

- consider the pre-work you want them to have done, if any (by having a 'trailer' or issuing a reading guide or handout for predigestion)

- consider the post-work you will want them to do (reading or 'finding out' tasks)

- choose your teaching aids: slides, overheads, video, or handouts

- discuss what you propose to do with the person who invited you to give the lecture, being prepared to modify it

- use pace and volume to emphasize your key points.

## Visual aids

### Slides

The arrival of photographic slides, and particularly of the carousel magazine, has damaged the craft of teaching, often reducing lectures to mere slide shows! (Having good slides is seen as an essential requisite and as a good reason for choosing a speaker, regardless of the validity of the message or the skill with which the topic is explained.) The basic idea, that learning is enhanced when information is provided through more than one channel, is of course sound but is vulnerable to overkill. Seeing a picture at the same time as hearing words enhances learning only when both are telling the same story and, even more importantly, providing the same category of information. As soon as they drift apart, learning is inhibited: the listener either concentrates on the words or the pictures or worse still flicks about between the two! Thus, talking about lesions while showing pictures of them is effective, as is describing a secular trend whilst showing a graph of incidence over time or enumerating risk factors while exhibiting a list of them on the screen. But if you move on from the lesions to the symptoms they cause, for which you have no pictures, while putting up more lesion pictures, your audience begins to suffer from 'intellectual strabismus'.

Too many slides reduce impact. At postgraduate level subtle differences between lesions or fine distinctions between slopes of graphs may be fascinating: at undergraduate level many slides of apparently the same subject are just confusing. Modern equipment has even given us the capability of having two pictures up at once: fine for, say, before and after shots, or comparing superficially similar but really significantly different pictures (the difference between ulcerative colitis and Crohn's for example), but if the two slides are not thus intimately related, dilution and strabismus are induced. A useful criterion is 'Could the pictures be meaningfully put on the same slide?'.

Not only do you not need a picture up all the time you are talking (and blank slides are less disturbing than keeping asking for 'Slide off' and 'Slide on'), there are times when you positively do not want one so that you can have the whole of their attention to make a crucial point. As the picture vanishes they start to look at you!

One of the problems about slide shows is that the lecturer spends a lot of the time looking not at the audience but at the screen, whether to use a pointer or only to satisfy himself that the slide he wanted is the one that is actually up. The cost is loss of eye contact with the audience and therefore loss of rapport. The speaker seems to be talking to the screen, not the listeners. There is another physical problem about using slides: the auditorium needs to be in semi- (and for some slides, total) darkness, which is neither conducive to note taking (which makes students cross) nor maintenance of the central excitatory state!

Slides can be divided into three types: pictures, diagrams, and lists (of which only the first cannot be put up as an overhead). Pictures (other than distracting fillers such as landscapes) are of lesions, of patients, or of images. The doctor with a clear mental picture of the expected signs, or of a possible lesion that could account for them, should generate good hypotheses as a basis for diagnosis. The nature of the lesion indicates the tests that can be done to confirm and assess the disease and the rationale for the treatment to be chosen. X-ray, ultrasound, and nuclear magnetic resonance images describe the lesion and define the capabilities of imaging in its investigation. Each picture shown should advance the argument: repeated pictures of the same thing, perhaps with minor variations, do not reinforce but dilute the impact. Parsimony is more effective than plethora!

Diagrams are a powerful tool for making connections, both between facts contained within the lecture and between facts in the lecture and those previously known to the listeners. As an example, a diagram of a biochemical pathway serves as a reminder of previously known material, and as a map on which the effects of pathophysiology can be explained. Graphs (whether lines, histograms, bar charts, or pie charts) are also powerful ways of presenting data, particularly when describing trends, contrasts, or patterns. Tables should be avoided at all costs: they nearly always present far too much data, and the audience will not have time to peruse them well enough to elicit the central message. If the crucial point derived from a table cannot be presented as a graph, it should not be presented visually but given in a handout for later perusal.

Almost any audience you address in medical education will be at home with the graphic presentation of data. Diagrams, however, have to be used with caution: about two thirds of any group of people have the sort of visual imagination that is helped by a good diagram, but the other third do not have an inherently visual imagination and can be confused by anything other than a well-drawn and simple one. Slides are not the ideal medium for diagrams since they tend to present too much information at one time. This can be offset by using a series of slides to build up the picture (for example, Slide 1 shows the endocrine organs; Slide 2 shows them with the efferent pathways; Slide 3 adds the afferent pathways).

Lists, whether of syndromes or risk factors or drugs for a condition, are beloved of students, who use them as a basis for revision and will always want them left on the screen long enough to copy them down, unless you have supplied them in a handout. If this happens – and obviously a long list (or a complicated diagram) takes time to copy down – your flow is interrupted and your pace dictated not by your evolving explanation but by your students' speed of writing, so consider this as a cost when deciding to use slides for lists. They are often used by lecturers as prompts or *aides-mémoire*, and can provide structure for the audience too. The current item under consideration can be coloured to establish which you are talking about. If this is done it is probably better to have a set of slides of the same list rather than trying to go back through the carousel to find it.

If you use a computer graphics package to generate bar graphs or pie charts, take a good look at the finished product. They offer their graphs 'in three dimensions', which may distort the facts on which they are based. This can be true when the columns on a bar chart or histogram are given 'depth', thereby suggesting volume of cases rather than simply number. It is particularly a problem with pie charts since, to provide the effect of three-dimensional perspective, the pie is rotated: the resultant perspective may distort the proportion of the various slices. Check this by seeing if the message appears to be the same when a key 'slice' is at 12 o'clock and when it is at 3 o'clock. See also the 'Rule of Eights' on page 20.

---

**Key points**

- The object of the exercise is not to show your slides but to use them to increase understanding.

- Too many slides reduce their impact.

- Slides can distract attention.

- Slides must support your explanation.

- Consider *why* you want each slide.

- Be parsimonious.

---

### Overhead transparencies

The overhead projector is a major teaching tool. It has three major characteristics which make it better than slides for everything except actual photographs: the lecturer can prepare it himself and therefore make sure that it will support his message; it does not require the audience to be kept in semi-darkness; and it can be layered up using overlays. Sadly, it is poorly used. At the most basic level, transparencies are badly prepared and therefore unreadable. Overheads are wrongly seen as less formal than slides, presumably because lecturers can make them for themselves, and at shorter notice, but this is no excuse for unprofessional scruffiness. Typically, overheads are unreadable because they rely on copies of typescript, or are handwritten in poor script, and often use colours which do not project well (yellow, brown, and orange cannot be read at all, and even red cannot be seen from well back). None of these failings is excusable. Today virtually everyone has access to a word processor on which there will be large type fonts which copy well on to overheads.

Another common failing is the use of a mask; the whole overhead is put up, but most of it is covered with a mask which is gradually removed. This is bad technique, which would become clear to its perpetrators if they reviewed their own lectures or sat in on other's because it upsets the audience's concentration. At best they spend more energy wondering what is under the mask than on listening to what the lecturer is saying, and at worst they feel cross because the lecturer does not seem to trust them or give them the credit for understanding the whole picture. This is doubly undesirable because the overhead is quintessentially a medium in which ideas can be built up a bit at a time.

Overheads can be used in three ways: fully prepared; partially prepared; and in real time. Fully prepared transparencies are carefully designed to convey a message in support of the lecturer's argument: content, layout, the use of colour, the need for overlays are worked out in plenty of time, and the finished article reviewed before use. Partially prepared transparencies are equally carefully designed, and the basic framework printed or written (legibly and in appropriate colours) in waterproof inks. While they are being projected, however, the lecturer adds further material in the preplanned places for impact (e.g. 'That's where this enzyme acts...' or 'This is where the blockage occurs...'). The added material can be in water-soluble ink so that it can be washed off and the basic framework used again. Real-time use of transparencies relies on the lecturer's ability to draw while talking about his subject! But given such ability (preferably practised and rehearsed beforehand), the technique has an immediacy which is very effective. The classic use of real-time overheads is by surgeons explaining a procedure ('That's the stomach, and we incise it there and join it to the ileum here like this...').

Overlays are the great and underused characteristic of overhead projection. A complex idea can be put over a bit at a time, each extra layer adding information to the basic framework. For example the first decision node on a flow chart is put up first, then the next, and so on. This allows the lecturer to concentrate on one step at a time without irritating his audience by masking. Written information, such as lists, can either be put up one group at a time, or the first transparency can show all the 'paragraph headings' in their appropriate place, and the overlays fill them in paragraph by paragraph. This is, incidentally, an ideal way of introducing a lecture by establishing the framework you propose to follow and adding material under each heading as you go along.

The tendency is always to overplay the visual aids. Not only do lecturers tend to use too many, thereby distracting from the essential core of their objective, but they tend to overload each slide or overhead. Layering overheads up reduces the overload, but even so the completed set may present the audience with information overload. The more slides or overheads you use (particularly those really belonging to another lecture), the more certain it is that some will be irrelevant. This is not neutral: irrelevant material gets in the way of learning because it is 'noise in the system', resulting in a high 'noise to signal ratio'. Educationalists have proposed the 'Rule of Eights':

- no more than eight slides/overheads per lecture
- no more than eight lines to a slide/overhead
- no more than eight words to a line
- every slide/overhead must be readable eight screen diameters away.

**Key points**

- Do not use typescript.
- Handmade overheads must be clearly printed.
- Do not use yellow, brown, or orange pens (and be wary of red in large theatres).
- Do not mask.
- Choose between fully prepared, partially prepared, and real-time overheads.
- Use overlays to build up an idea.
- Conform to the 'Rule of Eights'.

### Video recordings

These are a very difficult visual aid and are best avoided. The only thing for which they should be used is to illustrate some form of movement or behaviour where the moving image conveys more than a static picture would. There are four problems. The first is that most video recordings are poor quality, particularly if the need to record spontaneity has precluded the use of studio and properly trained technicians (not just cameramen but directors too). Remember that your audience is used to seeing television produced at enormous expense but with huge technical polish (whatever you think of the content). The second problem is that, except when you are on your own ground, you are dependent on unfamiliar equipment and strange technicians. Murphy's law applies: if anything can go wrong it will (and Murphy was an optimist!). The third problem is that the audience's attention span is short. Ten minutes is the absolute maximum for which they will watch attentively (no matter for how long they will watch TV at home). The fourth problem revolves around emotions and ethics. If you want to show the behaviour of people with disabilities, or for example different sorts of epilepti-form attacks, some people in the audience will feel embarrassed by becoming 'voyeurs' and others will worry about ethical issues such as whether your subject's consent was really informed, and about confidentiality.

If you do use video recordings, do it in short bursts. Show each sort of movement or behaviour separately and then talk about it (using the pause button), rather than the whole set in one burst. However much you want to emphasize a particular aspect, it is unwise to try to rewind and replay it, even if you have rehearsed it *on that particular video recorder* and noted the tape counter readings (no two counters are the same). Audiences get bored, embarrassed, or hilarious as the images whirl backwards, jabbering in a high pitch, and mixed with 'snowstorms'. You lose their concentration and, quite possibly, their respect. To emphasize a point, tell them *before* you play the tape what to watch out for, and afterwards reinforce it ('Did you all see him...') before going on to the next clip.

---

**Key points**

- Avoid video if you can.

- Rehearse it in the theatre you will be using it in.

- Use it in short bursts.

- Do not try to use replays.

- Make sure you are not open to criticism on ethical grounds.

---

### Handouts

Handouts serve two functions: supporting the lecture and facilitating revision. They can, therefore, be thought of in three phases: pre-work, current (or 'focus'), and post-work.

Pre-work handouts have to be distributed at a suitable interval before your lecture (only practicable if it is one in a series) to allow the participants to do the preparatory work you want. The handouts should start by stating your aims ('By the end of the lecture I want you to understand/ have grasped ... key principle...') and go on to suggest preparatory work such as selected references for reading (not too many!), or things that they should find out for themselves before they come ('Find out from a patient with X what it is like to...').

With the pre-work can go the material for use in the lecture itself. This is obviously efficient and can save paper (and it saves the undignified scrum at the beginning as the audience collects them) but Murphy's law suggests that at least some of the audience will have forgotten to bring it to the lecture (particularly at postgraduate level). It may be objected, particularly with reference to undergraduates, that if you give them the handouts beforehand they won't come to the lecture! Against this position it could be said that, as long as they learn what you want them to, it doesn't matter!

Current (or 'focus') handouts are for use during your lecture and therefore facilitate learning by focusing the learners' attention and minimizing distraction. Their most important function is to save the learner painstakingly copying down lists, diagrams, or graphs from your slides or overheads instead of listening to what you are saying about them. It also saves you the embarrassment of being asked to leave a slide up longer while they copy it down, and thereby compromising your pacing. As for pre-work handouts, it is good practice to start a handout with your aims. It helps your learners to think what they are supposed to get out of your lecture. It can even inform their questioning because they can appreciate which bits they have understood and what they haven't grasped and need help with.

Diagrams or graphs can be presented complete in the handout or unlabelled so that the learner adds to them as the lecture proceeds. Lists should be set out with plenty of room between lines or in one margin for the learner to annotate them. In this way handouts support at least some *active* learning during your lecture. Each diagram, graph, or list can be accompanied by a very short, pithy statement of its significance to reinforce what you have told them in your lecture. Handouts should not be used to carry large volumes of factual information.

Post-work, or revision aid, can be incorporated in handouts for current use or given out after the lecture. The main thing they take away will be the annotated lists, diagrams, and graphs, together with your pithy statements, which should provide the material for reflection on what you have taught them in the short term and revision for exams in the long term. Additional post-work will mostly be guided reading (references or reprints) but could include fact-finding tasks or problem-solving exercises.

Self-assessment packages are very well received but seldom used in medical education (probably because of scepticism that people can be trusted to mark themselves objectively, despite the evidence to the contrary). Self-assessment questions should not be multiple-choice question (MCQ) type, which only test factual recall, but should test understanding by setting problems ('When a patient presents with X what is the most important sign to look for and why?'; 'In a case of Y, what is the significance of test result Z? What action should be taken? What should the patient be told?'). Answers should be provided either on another page, in a sealed envelope, or printed upside down on the same page. It is entirely up to your listeners to use self-assessment, and it is important to make this clear. No one will collect their marks or enquire how they have done: this is *self*-assessment.

---

**Key points**

- Handouts must be designed to facilitate learning.

- They should set out the teacher's aims.

- They can suggest preparatory work to lay a foundation for a lecture.

- They can focus learning by providing a skeleton for note-taking.

- They save learners time in copying things down.

- They allow learners to concentrate on the teacher's message.

- They can guide subsequent learning.

- They can provide for self-assessment.

---

# Small-group work

Small-group work addresses two sorts of learning. In the cognitive or knowledge domain it provides active learning of intellectual skills (problem solving and decision making). This of course uses and therefore reinforces factual knowledge and can stimulate a need for more. In the attitudinal domain it allows learners to consider their feelings about the issues under discussion and compare them to those of their teacher and their peers. In either method, being like your peers is more important than being like your teacher!

Groups are composed of members: activity is by the members. The achievement of the aims of the session is by the members. As the teacher you should regard yourself as a member, with the same primary responsibility as the others to achieve the aims. What you have is a secondary responsibility to the group to help them do so. To signal your membership it is essential that you find out and use the group members' names, and make sure they know yours. One way of 'depowering' yourself is to use first names, getting theirs and signalling that they can use yours if they want to.

Small-group work aimed at learning in the cognitive domain will usually be *task orientated*. The group is presented with a problem or situation, together if necessary with some basic information, and is asked to come to an agreed course of action. In doing so they will pool their knowledge, thereby teaching each other. The importance of learning from one's peers is that there is no doubt that if they know something you should too, whereas what an expert puts over in a lecture may be something only relevant to his or her specialty or professional grade.

Small-group work aimed at fostering appropriate attitudes may be task orientated (by presenting the group with a problem to solve which engages their emotions) but can be *discussion based*. In the latter the group is presented with a general topic rather than a problem and is expected to come to an agreement as to the proper approach to it.

The essential dynamic of group work is that it gives the learner an opportunity to encapsulate his or her knowledge in a statement put forward for peer assessment ('I think that what happens is...'; 'I think that what should be done is...'). It has been said, perhaps tongue in cheek, that people in a group are not listening to what the others say but for a gap to make their own statements! The point is that you do not risk being looked down on by your colleagues, so you consider what you are going to say very carefully. That, in turn, means that you review all your knowledge of the topic, prioritize it in terms of its usefulness in this context, and achieve a synthesis, which is high-quality learning because you *use* knowledge rather than just having to accept it as in the passive learning in a lecture.

The role of the teacher in small-group work is twofold: to facilitate the members' exploration and use of information and to act as chairman. 'Facilitation' is to establish the topic to be discussed, to supply, occasionally, useful items of information and, when appropriate, help the discussion move towards greater sophistication ('OK, that's right. But what if...'). As the teacher you should do less talking than any one group member. If asked a direct question you can supply an answer or reflect the question back ('What do you think?' or 'Does anyone here know?'), but if you do supply the answer you should add a supplementary question so that the group members are not saved the trouble of thinking by your supplying information.

The chairmanship role has two tasks: to keep the group moving towards the aim of the session and to provide space for every member to have some input. The fact that the teacher is not acting as instructor does not mean that you do not have an aim: your choice of the topic on which the members are to work is based on what you want them to get out of it ('By the end of the session they will have understood that the crucial point is...'; 'By the end of the session they will have accepted that the clinician has a responsibility to...'). The group can lose its way and go off down blind alleys; it can, because it dislikes something you want it to face up to, retreat into chat; or it can be 'hijacked' by a member who wants it to address his or her personal agenda. When you see this happening you have two decisions to make: how long to let it go on for and, if you have to, how to get the group back on course. You can afford to let the group wander for a short while (not least because it may need to get its breath back after a particularly intense bit of work) and because you don't want always to be taking control. Often it will be a group member who lets you off the hook by drawing the members' attention to the fact that they are off course, and it is worthwhile waiting to see if this will happen. If you have to pull on the reins, try to do so as a member of the group ('Come on folks, we're off course...') rather than using the power that comes from your status ('You're wasting time...').

The other chairmanship task is to give everyone in the group a chance to have their say. Members remain silent for one of two main reasons. Some are out of sympathy with the group and/or the group process and are not prepared to pull their weight by contributing ideas and comments. Others are too timid to risk putting forward their ideas for peer review. Body language will usually indicate those with the first sort of attitude. You have a tactical choice. You can shame them into contributing ('Come on X, we haven't heard much from you. What do you think...?'). This runs the risk of being rebuffed or of losing group support (group members will usually club together to defend a colleague from the teacher) and thus wasting time or losing the group's momentum. Alternatively, you can let it go and write them off for the session. If you do, you should talk to them privately afterwards to sort out the problem, lest it continues to slow the group down next time. Again sometimes other members do it for you by attacking their failure to pull their weight. The member who is silent because he or she is too timid to put ideas forward may be naturally unassertive, or may previously have been mocked for an idea or statement. When you appreciate that someone is unduly quiet it is your job to 'make safe space' for them by indicating first that you value their ideas ('What about you, A? I'd value your ideas here') and secondly that you won't permit destructive criticism ('It's a difficult area, everyone has a right to their opinions. How do you feel, Y?' or 'I know this is not easy, it took me ages to understand. How do you see it, Z?'). Where necessary you may have to come down hard on a member who is being destructive ('That's enough, B. Everyone's got a right to their opinion...'). The longer a group is together the more trust between members is built up, and the more care they take of each other, so the less there is for the teacher to do in the chairmanship role.

All the above considerations apply equally to discussion groups which are aimed at attitude formation. Here the process is triggered by the presentation of a situation and behaviour within it as a basis for comment as to the propriety of what was done and the possibility that it could have been done better. This helps the learners to review their own and each others' feelings about what is proper, desirable, and ethical, not *in vacuo* but with regard to specific situations and instances. The teacher has the opportunity, however, to extend their conclusions from the particular to the general ('Well, if that's the right way of dealing with X, is it the right way of dealing with Y?').

---

**Key points**

- Group work uses active learning toward clearly defined aims.

- It enables learners to encapsulate their understanding for peer review.

- Task-orientated work is directed at cognitive (intellectual skills) learning.

- Discussion-based work is directed at attitudinal development (personal values).

- The teacher is a member of the group.

- The teacher has leadership and chairmanship responsibilities.

---

# Ward rounds

The ward round is traditionally the centrepiece of clinical learning, bringing into immediate proximity the needs of a real patient and the wisdom of the teacher. It underpins the apprenticeship component of medical education and gives the teacher the opportunity to provide instruction by both precept and example. It is the teaching occasion most likely to provide the learner with a role model. That model, however, will not necessarily be a positive one; and while negative role models are a useful influence on career development, no teacher wants to be one! While every qualified doctor can remember individual teachers and occasions that were a great learning experience, he or she can also remember others that were the opposite, often because of being, or seeing a friend, excoriated or humiliated by the teacher.

In its essence the ward round is an occasion when the teacher can do several things with the learner (whether a student or doctor in the training grades): you can test interpersonal and manual skills, review his or her ability to synthesize information from a variety of sources into a diagnostic hypothesis, assess the knowledge base that goes into that synthesis, and see if the ideas for investigation and treatment are sensible, humane, and economic. Two points emerge from that catalogue of learning opportunities. The first is the danger of unstructured teaching which can produce fuzziness in the learning ('I don't know what I was supposed to get out of that, and I don't know whether I got it'). The second is the inherently adversarial nature of the transaction; note the words above: 'test', 'review', 'assess' 'see if'. The dynamic is that the learner has to prove himself before you in public and is therefore, from the outset, defensive. (It is important to recognize that, unlike small-group work, statements have to be made not only in front of one's peers but others, such as the patients, and nurses. That is, not a 'trusting group'.) This inherent characteristic is reinforced by the Jesuitical style of teaching common to most consultants: error is exposed and corrected (and, if necessary, punished) as soon as it is recognized. This is in contrast to the heuristic style in which learners are allowed to continue in error until they recognize it for themselves (and, therefore, upbraid themselves). On ward rounds, more than anywhere else in medical education, the power imbalance between teacher and learner is out in the open. To undergraduates the teacher may soon be a clinical examiner; to the young doctor the writer of references. In an adversarial situation with a built-in power imbalance, the learning opportunities are often missed in the need to defend one's self.

Both the above dangers can be minimized by well thought out teaching. In the selective ward round, where only a few patients' problems are addressed, cases can be picked to teach selected lessons, and used in a rational sequence. It is just as important to have defined your aims before a ward round as it is before a lecture. It is not *ad hoc* and you are not entirely dependent on the available clinical material (by which you mean the sick people under your care!). For each available patient you can choose what to concentrate on, whether it be neurological examination, occupational history, differential diagnosis, rational investigation, or the relative safety, effectiveness, acceptability, and economy of the different treatments available. Even in the full ward round (and, for teaching training grades, work rounds), if you know the patients on the ward you can define your educational aims for each. You have, of course, a strategic choice: on any specific round you can choose whether to concentrate on one issue, which has the benefit of showing how basic skills contribute to every patient's care; or to progress from one skill to the next in the pantheon, history taking, physical examination, hypothesis formation and testing, or therapeutics. The latter has, of course, the advantage that you can show how they all fit together. Your choice will depend largely on where your learners are in their career: getting each skill right before going on to the next is desirable early in the course, getting it all together essential later on.

Avoiding the worst effects of the adversarial nature of ward-round teaching depends on the adoption of a collegial approach. After all, the people you are teaching are already your junior colleagues, or soon could be. Knowing your students' first names and using them helps. So does consideration of the words you use. So much of our professional interaction is adversarial that we have lost sight of its impact on lesser mortals. We say 'Didn't you think of...?' and 'Why didn't you...?' and 'Why not...?' and 'Don't you know that...?'. You can almost see the minatory finger jabbing towards you as you read those words! Try 'What did you think...?'; 'What were your options?'; 'What are the possibilities?'; and 'How much do you know about...?'. Semantically the differences are small, but on the receiving end they are considerable. This fits in with a 'problem-based' approach to clinical teaching which starts by describing the patients' problems in their terms, then discusses what we need to know to address those problems, then reviews what we do know, then agrees how to find out what we need but don't know, and so on.

Ward rounds are an ideal opportunity to achieve synthesis between basic science and clinical practice. Think of every case as an opportunity to review the relevant bioscience and relate it to the phenomena under review. The tendency is to ignore the underlying science and work in the area of diseases and their management, but this, if persisted with, leaves the learner with the idea that bioscience was not important and does not need to be kept under review. Faced, for example, with a confused patient, one approach is to list the syndromes in which confusion features. This inculcates a problem-solving approach based on going through a list and excluding each disease on it until diagnosis is made by exclusion. The weakness of this approach (common among candidates for membership of the Royal College of Physicians) is that it precludes the diagnosis of a condition not on the list or forgotten from it. A better approach is to consider confusion as brain failure, and to discuss what a brain needs to function properly. Each item on that list then prompts consideration of what might deprive the brain of it, and from that a range of enquiries to be initiated. Even if the learner has not heard that myxoedema can affect brain function, he or she can see that, since thyroxine is needed for normal brain activity, the stigmata of hypothyroidism need to be looked for, and thyroid function tested. This approach enables the learner effectively to diagnose conditions they have never heard of, and will result in their continued interest in biological sciences whose relevance they have now experienced at first hand.

Making the learner commit himself is sometimes inescapable. If you are told that the ankle jerk is present, or the spleen enlarged, or there are exudates on the retina, it is all too easy to convince yourself that those were your findings too! It is your responsibility to make sure that the necessary skills are in place by the completion of the teaching for which you are responsible, and the only way of doing it is to present the learner with such a challenge, observe the result, and give him or her feedback. Nevertheless, how that is done can make all the difference between a good and a bad learning experience. The student who is frightened of being shown to be incompetent, and particularly the student who cannot bear to lose face, will adopt defensive tactics. At best this will consist of staying at the back of the group, avoiding eye contact with you, and trying to get out of presenting the case or demonstrating the skills you want to see. At worst such students absent themselves from ward rounds altogether (sometimes comforting themselves with the idea that it is more important for getting through exams to read the books than 'waste time on the wards'). So, to avoid this type of behaviour on your rounds, don't make theatre out of it! Wrap it up in your teaching: 'What will we find if there is an upper motor neurone lesion on that side? Jane, see if you can elicit that reflex' is better than 'Let's see if you can get an ankle jerk'. Similarly, 'There's a better way to do it. Let me show you' is better than 'You're wrong. Go and learn how to do it'. Treat your learners like colleagues, minimize the extent to which negative feedback constitutes loss of face, and they will submit more cheerfully and less defensively.

## Key points

- Ward round teaching addresses explicit aims.
- Cases should be chosen and sequenced to achieve those aims.
- Ward rounds should facilitate active learning.
- The phenomena encountered should be related to basic science rather than, or as well as, diagnostic entities.
- Teacher–learner interaction should avoid being adversarial.
- A problem-based approach is effective.
- Heuristic is better than Jesuitical teaching.

- The learners' dignity should be protected.
- The relationship between teacher and learner should be collegial.

## One-to-one tutorial

This is a difficult form of teaching: with undergraduates the power differential is overwhelming; with doctors in the training grades the shift from collegial to pupil role and status is uncomfortable for both teacher and learner.

The aim of any tutorial is to help the learner crystallize his or her understanding of a topic. The teacher wants to make sure that the learner really understands the subject in depth. The tendency is for the learner to seek to keep it at a level of complexity with which he can cope; it is the teacher's responsibility to reveal the underlying complexity and guide the learner through it and, where necessary, face up to the gaps in the knowledge needed so that uncertainty can be coped with reasonably. In other words, you build on your learner's basic knowledge by sharing your hard-won wisdom. Since the wisdom gap is probably commensurate with the power gap, so that the learner despairs of ever attaining your status, your depowering strategy can be focused on your uncertainty. (To pretend that you know everything about a subject is to ask to be caught out!) The brighter your pupil the more you can share your recognition of the limitations of our understanding.

For these reasons tutorials should not be used simply to review basic knowledge of common topics (where the adversarial nature of that task, together with the pupil's lack of supporting peers, would make the interaction intensely uncomfortable). Essentially they should take the form of a joint exploration of a complex problem to which each participant brings something: the learner his or her preparatory work, the teacher experience and the sense of proportion that comes from it. That is not to say that the teacher need not prepare for a tutorial. As for every other type of teaching you must have your aims clear in your head (or down on paper) before you start. With your aims clear you select the topic and the way it is presented. You can expect your pupil to read it up, but the old dodge of saying 'You teach me about X' is not acceptable! If the learner reads the standard texts and peruses the mainstream references, the teacher should be prepared to read around the subject, doing some 'lateral thinking' with the aim of widening the learner's vision when the two sets of preparation are brought together.

Of course, the agenda is not always set by the teacher. The learner may ask you for help in a specific area which he finds difficult. This is simpler, and of course you have a clear mandate to teach. Even so, the power gap and the danger of adversarialism can threaten the process. The pupil has opened by admitting a weakness: the teacher's role is to help. The first need is to assess the real nature of the problem for which the learner has asked for help. 'I need some help with X' can mean a perceived lack of knowledge, of intellectual skill, of manual or procedural skill, or an emotional response that impedes decision making.

---

**Key points**

- The aim of a tutorial is to help the learner crystallize his or her understanding.

- Tutorials are inappropriate for simply reviewing knowledge.

- The task of the teacher is to reduce uncertainty in areas of complexity.

- While the learner prepares longitudinally, the teacher prepares laterally.

- When the learner sets the agenda the teacher must elucidate the real needs.

---

## Summary

- All teaching should have clear aims, addressing learning in the domains of cognition, skill, and feelings.

- A teacher should always know where his or her teaching fits the overall learning pattern of the pupils.

- Teaching should be designed in recognition of the learners' feelings, particularly the effects of the perceived power imbalance between teacher and taught.

- Medical teachers must aim to be as professional as teachers as they are as clinicians.

- Given the aims, a teacher should adopt the most effective methods of meeting them, but given the method (being invited to teach in a specific way), a teacher must select the most achievable aims.

- All other things being equal, the teacher should always opt for methods which promote active learning.

- The teacher should provide passive learning (e.g. lectures) in such a way that it will provoke and facilitate active learning.

- Teachers should use aids parsimoniously, and choose them in terms of their probable contribution to specific aims.

- Medical teachers should respect their learners as people who will be their colleagues in due course.

# 3 Teaching facts and developing attitudes

## Tim Dornan

## Introduction

Progress up the medical hierarchy brings with it responsibility for teaching, whether of undergraduates, junior doctors, or fully trained doctors undertaking continuing medical education (CME). Sooner or later most doctors will be expected to teach, and to teach well, regardless of the fact that they may have had no training for the task.

Faced with such a challenge many fall back on the strategy of passing on their large store of factual knowledge, attested to by the letters after their names – skills they see as being learned 'on the hoof' or 'by osmosis'. The idea that they have responsibility for their learners' attitudes may be regarded with suspicion, at best as psycho-social interference, at worst as brainwashing. A simple way out is to say 'Anyway, you can't teach attitudes'. Facts, on the other hand, are safe. They have a lot of them, their learners have few, and therefore they are in a comfortingly powerful position.

Over-reliance on factual transfer, underteaching of intellectual skills (decision making and problem solving), abrogation of the responsibility for juniors' attitudes, and the abuse of power are common weaknesses in conventional medical education. In this chapter, the following questions are addressed:

- Are 'facts' what we should be aiming to teach?
- Can you actually 'teach' them?
- If so, how?
- How do facts measure up beside other educational priorities?
- How do you decide what attitudes should be 'developed'?

- Is it the teacher or the learner that 'develops' them?

If your question is 'How can I teach what they need to know to be competent?', this chapter will help by redefining it as 'How can I help them learn to be competent?'. It explores how that redefines your task as a 'teacher' and how you might accomplish the task in several common educational settings. It explores what the term 'attitudes' encompasses and how you can use the relationship with your learners to 'develop' them, particularly through role modelling and appraisal. The main premises are that you should:

- help the learner learn rather than 'teach'

- improve understanding rather than factual recall

- build competence which is an amalgam of skills, attitudes, and experience as well as knowledge

- teach in the workplace and use day-to-day experience as your starting point as much as possible.

## Learner-centredness

Chapters 1 and 2 have emphasized the basic educational principle that adults learn best by:

- having their interest aroused

- identifying their learning needs

- being responsible for their learning

- building on previous learning.

Why does so much medical education breach these principles? Most postgraduate learners have only experienced pedagogic, spoon-feeding approaches in their undergraduate training. Clinical hierarchies and postgraduate training structures encourage learners to see themselves as children more than adults. Adult learning is demanding of concentration and effort; it is more comfortable to learn passively. Pedagogic teaching has attractions for the teacher as well as the learner because it puts the teacher in a position of power. It allows him to determine the subject matter and avoid exposing his own uncertainty and ignorance. Comfortable though this relationship may appear to both parties, it is neither efficient nor effective. Much effort is wasted in preparing and delivering ineffective teaching.

## Learners as people

The teacher must recognize that no two learners have the same level of understanding or learning needs. Effective teaching recognizes this, identifies the correct starting point, and progresses at the learner's own pace. Far from diminishing the teacher, letting the learner set the pace enhances efficiency and builds a relationship which can bring the teacher his greatest rewards.

Quite apart from their heterogeneous intellectual abilities and states of knowledge, learners vary in how they react to the context in which they are learning. Students in their last year at school are an élite who have been given a place to train in one of the most competitive careers. In their first university year they find themselves at the bottom of the pile with no status or responsibility. They have to struggle with a mountain of new knowledge. No wonder they are brittle and vulnerable. Likewise, the new clinical student is in an unfamiliar environment confronting difficulties from which he has previously been sheltered. These include the practical challenges of medical practice, ethical dilemmas and the emotional impact of pain, fear, anger, disfigurement, and death. The senior house officer suddenly finds himself the senior member of the cardiac arrest team. The registrar is taking new responsibilities in the out-patient clinic. All of these contexts may be taken for granted by the teacher but can undermine confidence. The teacher can make a valuable contribution by acknowledging, discussing, and 'legitimizing' the feelings which these situations engender so that confidence is boosted and learning can proceed.

## Knowledge and competence

Both the consultant who asks a student on the ward round for 'the ten causes of...' and the Royal College which gatekeeps higher medical training with a multiple-choice examination of factual exotica are giving the same message: facts are power. However, there is more to doctoring than knowledge. We have all come across knowledgeable doctors who are ineffective because they do the wrong things, are practically inept, or upset their colleagues. On the other hand, one cannot deny that good motivation and the best skills are wasted without sound understanding. Effective education must recognize the acquisition of knowledge as just one of several goals. The challenge is to integrate it with skills and attitudes.

The starting point of clinical practice is 'a patient with a problem'. If learning has the same starting point, knowledge, skills, and attitudes fall into place beside one another. The educational challenge is to analyse each clinical problem in such a way as to define the attitudes, knowledge, and skills which can be learned from it. Medicine is essentially practical; we spend our professional lives 'doing'. Apprenticeship allows integrated learning reinforced by concern about the welfare of others, which is the substance of our profession and the reward of partnership with professional colleagues. Helping the learner learn from experience in the workplace develops true professional competence rather than the disintegrated components of competence.

# Acquisition of knowledge

## A 'syllabus' of knowledge?

There are two ways of defining the knowledge content of an educational curriculum. One, much favoured by learners, is a 'syllabus' or exhaustive list of content. The other can be described as the 'spine and ribs' model. There is a spine of understanding which every learner must acquire for basic competence, but that is by no means all a learner should aim for. How far and along which rib the learner goes is determined by his or her curiosity and motivation. For example, one might wish to study the molecular biology of autoimmunity while another learner studies the epidemiology of diabetes in ethnic minorities.

Popular though they are with learners, syllabuses have problems. They can be dauntingly large and demotivate learning by circumscribing the knowledge base. By implication, topics which are not listed should not be learned (even if they are interesting) and all within the syllabus are of equal importance. As often as not, learners acquire their syllabus from a favoured textbook which presents a mass of factual knowledge without prioritizing it. Examinations have a lot to answer for since they often achieve discriminatory power by testing knowledge which is of little practical value (reliability at the expense of validity). Passing or failing people on performance at the boundaries of their knowledge has two drawbacks: it encourages a 'syllabus mentality' and puts more emphasis on the fringe (the rarely encountered) than the centre (the commonplace). Doctoring, on the other hand, demands an excellent command of the commonplace supported by an ability to recognize that a situation is unfamiliar and react to it. In this way, we constantly refine and expand our understanding and knowledge of the commonplace and the rare.

The teacher's task is made much easier if he discards the concept of 'syllabus', equips learners with the skills to refine and understand their knowledge, and uses his own experience and understanding to help them define their 'core' of knowledge and build on it. The process of defining the core is of educational value if it is done 'live' with the learners, as is possible in seminars or tutorials. This can be undertaken by thinking in terms of practical problems. Taking the example of acute chest pain, the knowledge base needed to deal with the commonplace and the rare could be encompassed by aiming for learners:

- to understand the pathophysiology, symptoms, and signs of ischaemic heart disease, its investigation, and treatment

- to understand how other common disease processes can cause acute chest pain, the clinical features which distinguish them, and their management

- to recognize that there are many other disorders which may cause acute chest pain and the clinical pointers towards some of these alternative diagnoses.

In this way, Dressler's syndrome and Bornholm disease could be covered but in their proper perspective.

Specialists planning to teach their discipline to generalist trainees should start by asking themselves the question 'What are the key things that any competent doctor should be able to do and what understanding is needed to achieve this?'. The result may be a key message such as that 'testing the urine of newly presenting diabetic patients for ketones is essential to pick out those who need insulin'. Learners should examine the pathophysiological and practical reasons why this message is important. Whatever is forgotten afterwards, the message is likely to stick. 'Nuggets of wisdom' sometimes have their place, especially if they help you understand rather than just remember. We all have a stock of our mentors' aphorisms and very useful they are too. The ability to pass on hard-won wisdom is a great strength of apprenticeship learning.

Defining what does *not* need to be learned is difficult because a justification can be found for teaching almost any piece of knowledge. One answer is to define the knowledge base by thinking of practical performance as the end-point of education. If a situation is unlikely to arise, harm is unlikely to come through not recognizing it and if appropriate referral will ensure that the problem is detected, little is to be lost by omitting it. Here is an example of where teaching a *skill* (referral practice) will produce a better practitioner than teaching *knowledge* which is likely to atrophy from disuse. This approach will also keep important rarities in the educational core. For example, congenital adrenal hyperplasia is an uncommon disease cared for exclusively by endocrinologists. However, failure to recognize a salt-losing crisis in a neonate with ambiguous genitalia will be fatal.

## Levels of understanding

The term 'facts' portrays acquisition of knowledge at its lowliest, very much a task for personal study. Teachers should set their sights higher. By helping learners understand and by identifying and removing intellectual obstacles, teachers can leave the facts to take care of themselves. Given the high entry requirements for medical school, medical students and doctors have the capacity for loftier intellectual activities. Teachers can help learners interpret data (including clinical cases), analyse situations, synthesize different pieces of learning into a greater understanding, and evaluate evidence. Teaching at this level is most likely to stick and most likely to influence behaviour and performance. It is also the most stimulating and rewarding. If you think back to your own training, you will probably best remember the teachers who helped you understand, interpret, and use information. None of this is possible without a learner-centred approach because difficulties in understanding, interpreting, synthesizing, and evaluating are highly individual. That is why it is so difficult to give a good lecture and why different members of the audience have such different views about the value of a particular lecture.

## Conceptual frameworks

Clinical medicine as a whole and the disciplines within it have their own underpinning frameworks and a task for the teacher is to help the learners see the framework into which items of data can be placed and integrated. As well as enhancing understanding, this enables students to extend their knowledge into other, related areas. I will illustrate this from my own discipline, endocrinology. The concept of feedback loops controlling hormone secretion underpins the pathophysiology, investigation, and treatment of endocrine disease. Having grasped that principle, the learner does not need to remember in isolation that the dose of thyroxine has to be titrated against the plasma concentrations of thyroxine and thyroid stimulating hormone (TSH) in primary hypothyroidism but can see these facts as part of a greater picture. He should not find it too difficult to remember that the adrenal gland is controlled by two major feedback loops and apply that understanding to the investigation and management of adrenal disease. Later in his career, the same concept will help him understand why a 'feedback tumour' could arise when the thyroid gland fails and the pituitary is continuously overproducing the trophic hormone, TSH. The feedback concept also explains why such a tumour regresses when hormone replacement therapy is optimized. Similarly, a junior student may find it helpful to think of heart failure in terms of what is needed to make the heart function normally (fuel, an intact 'engine' and valves, and appropriate pressures in the input and output lines). It is only a short step from there to understand the rationale for diuretic, nitrate, vasodilator and inotropic therapy, and valve replacement in the management of heart failure. Never be afraid of being simple and basic, as long as you do not patronize your learners because, once the underlying principle is securely in place, they can build on it.

If you are working at the level of factual knowledge, exceptions to rules are inconvenient data which have to be remembered. If you work at the level of principles, exceptions can be used to broaden out understanding in a way which makes them hard to forget.

## Language

Nothing is better at making a person an 'outsider' than jargon. At worst, it is a way of dressing up simple concepts in confusing terminology. However, terms may be a useful shorthand loaded with meaning, in which case familiarity with language aids understanding. Terms may be confusing if they are used differently in different situations. In this case, sloppy language leads to poor understanding or misconceptions and clarifying definitions will help to integrate knowledge. The first contribution a teacher can make is himself to use simple, clear terminology and know what he means by it. The second is to test learners' understanding, correct misconceptions, and agree common usage. The third is to encourage a questioning attitude to both the use and meaning of language. So, for example, you cannot learn endocrinology without understanding the term 'hormone'; exploring understanding of the term is a good way into the clinical discipline and can be used to draw basic science learning into clinical practice.

## Intellectual skills and acquiring knowledge

The primary objective is that the learner should make sensible decisions, i.e. exercise intellectual skill. While this needs knowledge, the real challenge is to:

- select the right facts from his/her memory bank
- synthesize these facts with the facts of the case
- work out a plan to test the accuracy of his/her interpretation.

Knowledge is not, therefore, the be-all and end-all of education. The message for the teacher is that learning by analysing real or hypothetical problems is always well received and puts into practice the problem-solving skills needed in everyday practice. It is a strange irony that rote-learning of basic sciences in the undergraduate curriculum is being swept aside by 'problem-based learning' whilst many clinical teachers forsake their problem-orientated clinical practice for a pedagogic style of teaching. How to make best use of clinical problems is considered in the next section.

## Specific situations

## The lecture

This presents the greatest challenge because it has to cater for all needs without any interaction. The lecturer's task is to 'explain' rather than 'tell'. If the teacher is to have any help from the learners, it has to be at the stage of preparation. It is good educational practice to involve learners early by asking them what they find hardest to get to grips with or what they would most like covered. From this and your own view of the topic come the educational objectives for your lecture, i.e. the 'take-home messages'. Learners rate good preparation more highly than entertainment value and are very canny at recognizing it. A simple discipline is to set yourself a preparation deadline some way ahead of the teaching date. A counsel of perfection is to ask a sample of the learners to look at your written material or listen to a rehearsal of your lecture. They will be good at picking up lack of clarity or points which need emphasis.

The skill of giving a lecture is to hold the attention of all despite their heterogeneity. One way of doing this is to punctuate it with 'gathering points' between sections (a pause, summary, joke, or provocative statement) to relax the intellectual tension, bring all the audience back together, and indicate that what was just said was a 'take-home message'. In written material, having good structure and layout achieves the same end, allowing more sophisticated learners to skip over material which they can easily identify as familiar. The adage about writing papers – say what you're going to say, say it, and then say what you've said – applies equally to lecturing although you have to be able to paraphrase skilfully to enhance understanding and prevent the repetition becoming irritating.

## Ward rounds

Ward rounds provide an excellent opportunity for learner-centred interactive teaching in small groups. Take, for example, a patient with chest pain. Learners are likely to know most of the background facts but may need some others to be filled in by the teacher. The facts can be used to formulate a differential diagnosis which leads to investigation and treatment strategies. The task of the teacher is to draw out knowledge and identify gaps, integrate that knowledge to enhance understanding, and apply it to a situation which is, by its nature, 'relevant' and likely to be remembered. Learners can be helped to identify gaps in their knowledge and fill them in their own time. This knowledge will have been more effectively and enjoyably acquired than if it were 'taught' in the abstract.

Ward rounds are not the only context in which problem-orientated, active learning can be conducted and they have the drawback that they are dictated by the case-mix available at the time, have to accommodate a mix of knowledge ranging from the senior registrar to the junior student nurse, and must take account of patients' sensitivities.

## Seminars

This is another situation where the teacher is well placed actively to help learners learn. The keynote for successful use of small groups is to define and build on the learners' existing knowledge base. So, for example, a group of apprehensive undergraduate students meeting a teacher for the first time for a seminar on the subject of 'stroke' might be asked to spend five minutes as a group (perhaps with the teacher out of the room) defining what they understand by the term and listing what they would like to know about it. The seminar might then progress from:

- defining terms, to

- exploring key concepts, to

- covering detailed factual information, to

- drawing the information together as approaches to clinical situations, and

- summarizing the points which have been covered.

The teacher is, of course, a resource but his primary role is to get the learners thinking, talking amongst themselves, and asking questions which help them define what they know and need to know. An important outcome of such a seminar is to define the gaps in knowledge to be filled in by private study.

Unfortunately, an adversarial approach to teaching is the rule more than the exception. Every question is an accusation ('What do you know about...?'; 'Let's see if you know any more than the usual St Elsewhere's student about...'). Learning is all too often painful and learners spend much of the time trying to look inconspicuous and not to commit themselves. Small semantic differences make large differences in students' perceptions and behaviour. 'What were the possibilities?', 'What options did you have?', and 'I'd like to hear how much you know about...?' are more learner-friendly ways of phrasing your questions. Learners will be readier to join in and you will attain deeper levels of discussion. If a session is not going well, consider whether you are working on the right 'stratum' of knowledge; it is quite possible that you have taken something for granted which underpins what you are talking about and none of your learners understand. Mixed ability groups can be a problem but a skilled teacher can use the heterogeneity of learners to advantage; what is the difference between learner A who seems to be with you and learner B who clearly is not? A can be asked to talk through a topic and then the teacher can check B, C, and D's understanding of it, perhaps by asking them to apply it.

## One-to-one teaching

Because the learner is alone with you, it is even more important not to dominate. This is particularly likely to happen if learning is conducted at the level of factual recall. It must work at the level of intellectual skills and be kept as collegial as possible: 'Let's work out what we can do for Mr X'. Positive feedback is essential: 'Good idea, but in this case you might find...'. Apart from discussing individual patients, asking the learner to tackle a hypothetical or real clinical problem or talk through the answers to a multiple-choice questionnaire are useful formats. The teacher must use every means at his disposal to make the learner feel safe in exposing his 'ignorance'.

## Self-directed learning

Almost your most important task is to encourage learning in your absence. Encourage learners to identify learning needs from the situations they encounter. Suggest some work in preparation for a seminar or lecture and 'debrief' the learners on the day but always encourage the learners to define the questions rather than do so yourself.

Advising about resource material is another responsibility of the teacher. As learners progress through their careers, the range of resource material and learning opportunities widens. For teachers of undergraduate students, knowing a range of textbooks, recommending sources such as educational videos or colour atlases, and encouraging students to read editorials and review articles in general medical journals may help to make learning more palatable and interesting. For postgraduate learners, the scope is wider and may extend to the choice of career moves or courses of study. One way or another, the teacher's role is to facilitate active and (ideally) enjoyable learning and counteract the belief that wisdom equates with passing exams and comes from ploughing slavishly through large tomes.

## Tricks

No matter how effectively learning is approached from theoretical principles, some individual items of data have to be retained. Take, for example, the side-effects of drugs. Some may be based on principles (as, for example with anti-arrhythmic agents) but others are idiosyncratic or based on principles so obscure that they are best regarded as isolated data. It is here that acronyms, associations, and alliterations come in. Humour has its place in medical teaching and banter in seminars or rounds may help to make information stick when all else fails (though this should not be at the expense of patients or learners). Touch and posture can also be used. A group of students in my own year had such difficulty remembering the myotomal values of the muscle groups in the legs that we devised a chant, complete with motions. I still use it (silently and motionless) today. That is not to suggest that you should surrender your dignity and turn your tutorials into a game of charades but you might ask if anyone in your tutorial group has thought of a way of remembering difficult facts. Visual imagery may be valuable (dermatomes, for example) and diagrams may be easier to remember than bald facts (biochemical pathways and the vectors of the ECG, for example).

## Study skills

The teacher has a responsibility to help learners learn to learn. The seasoned clinician will have developed so much self-sufficiency in his practice (and learning) that he may not even entertain this thought. However, the educational background and personal development of the learners may not have prepared them to take responsibility for their own education. They may see a yawning gap between the clinical material encountered on the wards and the theory of structure and function taught years before. Even clinical practice and factual clinical knowledge may be seen as divorced from one another. The teacher's role is to find out the learner's approach to learning, help him/her recognize and reconcile the different modes of learning, and encourage a spirit of enquiry. Rote learning and slavish burning of midnight oil may need to be discouraged in favour of dipping frequently into a wide range of source materials.

## The importance of attitudes

If acquisition of factual information is the most overemphasized aspect of medical education, development of attitudes is the most neglected. Attitudinal objectives do not lend themselves to testing in a 'true/false' format and may be seen as nebulous. Consider, however, how far attitudes towards colleagues, patients, and society in general influence professional performance. In addition, the importance of attitude towards learning itself has been stressed in the earlier part of this chapter.

## Setting and monitoring attitudinal objectives

Attitudinal learning is sometimes regarded as an 'unwritten agenda' in medical education but, for it to have the emphasis it deserves, it should be explicit. For example, good performance in the care of acute myocardial infarction might be achieved by a learning objective such as:

The doctor will have the attitude that it is his/her responsibility to ensure that all patients with suspected acute myocardial infarction receive fibrinolytic therapy after due explanation with minimal delay.

In this case, the emphasis is not so much on the skill of successful fibrinolytic therapy or the knowledge of when it is indicated as on the willingness to get out of bed in a hurry, explain the situation patiently, and ensure successful implementation.

Performance objectives such as punctuality, efficiency, and considerate behaviour may be hard to define and measure but are reasonably easy to recognize. They reflect attitudes and are likely to figure prominently in the appraisal of staff in training. Agreeing performance/attitudinal objectives at the start of a period of training allows these attributes to be put in place beside knowledge and skills. It will come as no surprise to the learner to be told that an area of factual knowledge is required of him or that he has to become competent at a practical skill, but the idea that punctuality, efficiency, and self-criticism are essential for good doctoring may not be taken for granted. Appraisal is particularly important to attitude development. From the learner's point of view, it is not too difficult to find out whether or not you know something or are competent at a practical skill but self-assessment of attitudes is difficult. Despite agreeing on a form of words as an attitudinal objective, a learner may have difficulty seeing how it fits into his practice. He may also underestimate his performance. Appraisal gives an excellent opportunity for encouraging good performance and, if sensitively handled, examining specific examples of poor performance.

For the teacher to agree these objectives and then not demonstrate them himself is silly. Role modelling and 'learning by example' are so central that attitude development provides a spur to the teacher to look to his own performance. It is for just this reason that medical education is inseparable from high-quality clinical practice. Someone who is unprepared to set an example should question his position as a teacher.

## Attitudes towards learning

Doctors who qualified 30 years ago and are now coping adequately with AIDS and information technology can do so because they absorbed the attitude that they must keep up to date. Today's graduates will be incompetent in ten years if they do not share that attitude. Continuing medical education is a contractual obligation for fully qualified doctors and is another area where role modelling can have either a positive or negative effect. The consultant who arranges his private session at a time which prevents him ever attending 'grand rounds' is spelling out a clear message to his trainees and is in no position to insist that his junior staff attend. By contrast, demonstrating a lively interest in current medical literature in case discussions or willingness to use new treatment strategies shows the trainee that even his ageing senior has retained the capacity to change with the times; friendly competition in quoting relevant literature is a healthy way of encouraging a spirit of enquiry, provided the chief allows himself to be upstaged at least some of the time.

## Relationship of attitudes to knowledge and skills

If poor performance in the domains of knowledge and skills is taken at face value, it is easy to write off a learner as unintelligent or inept and offer them no useful help. Often, an attitudinal problem underlies poor performance. Identifying the problem allows a far better assessment of the learner's potential and leads to more effective solutions. The problem may be career uncertainty, lack of confidence, disillusionment, depression, or emotional isolation. The responsibility is on the mentor to look below the surface of poor performance.

## Personal qualities of the teacher and learner

This discussion has so far concentrated on those attitudes which are most tangible and most closely related to clinical performance. Stepping back from individual case management and considering the attributes of the best doctors you have known will show the importance of idealism, unselfishness, dedication, and willingness to become involved with patients. If punctuality is hard to 'teach', an attribute like unselfishness is a great deal harder but both can be learned. Here, the apprenticeship model assumes its full importance. Favourable qualities which the learner brings to his/her training can be encouraged and unfavourable ones discouraged. New attitudes can be implanted and nurtured. Trainers must be aware that the positions they occupy, what they stand for, who they are, and what they do influences their trainees every bit as much as explicit 'teaching'. They are well placed to inspire or disappoint, encourage or disillusion. The teacher must keep constantly at the back of his mind his position as a role model and the attitudes he wishes to develop in his trainees. He must allow this awareness to influence his behaviour.

The teacher's attitudes may also affect his effectiveness in teaching knowledge and skills. Learners often say that the best teacher is one who is enthusiastic about his/her subject and able to transmit the enthusiasm. Some have the opposite effect! Encouraging and rewarding interest, building confidence, and helping learners to realize the importance of what they are studying all aid learning. A teacher whose students go home inspired to find out more about the subject will achieve far more than one who slavishly rehearses a syllabus.

Unfortunately, clinical life is rarely smooth but there are ways in which the trainer's behaviour can turn even difficulties to advantage: apologizing for irrational behaviour, explaining irascibility and how the trainee contributed to it, being prepared to admit mistakes, or climbing down from postures strengthens the bond between trainer and trainee and teaches the all-important attitudes of self-criticism and willingness to accept fallibility. I also believe that inviting learners to visit you in your own home and meet your family can have a similar effect if it is relaxed and informal. The most unpalatable aspect of role modelling is that there are respects in which you will be used by your trainees as a negative model. Since all teachers have different strengths, there will always be respects in which you are weaker than other teachers. You must accept this inevitability and not try to be all things to all people; comfort yourself that your learner's comment 'at least he has no pretentions about his ability to . . .' is, ultimately, positive!

A large part of the teacher's task is to know his own attitudes and those he wishes his learners to develop. Beyond that, the more discretely he 'teaches' his apprentices the better. An attitude imposed by authority risks being rejected; the sensitive learner will, provided the learning environment and peer group are right, find his own way and the teacher may have to bite his tongue nine times out of ten when he encounters attitudes he does not share. I am a believer in speaking very plainly on the tenth occasion. If you have a good relationship with your learner and are normally restrained in criticizing his/her attitudes, a clear statement that you disagree with an attitude or, more likely, an action which flows from it will have a powerful effect if you use this power sparingly and with a strong sense of responsibility.

## Attitudes to patients

What distinguishes medicine from other professions is, above all else, the intimate knowledge the doctor has of his patients and the power he has over them. If the case is simple and the doctor–patient relationship easily established, clinical care is plain sailing. There are times, however, when neither obtain. True professionalism demands an approach to patients which transcends personal likes and dislikes and prejudices. These values should figure large in the training agenda and be modelled by the teacher. A discussion of resistant or unattractive patients allows the teacher to explore the learner's reactions, show that he also feels unfavourable emotions, and discuss how he copes with them. Sharing emotions provoked by difficult clients has the additional effect of helping team-building and the benefits to learning which come from it.

## The context of learning

Whether in hospital or primary care, the trainer has responsibility to provide a good learning environment. Good staff relationships, efficiency, humanity, and a patient-orientated approach will rub off on the learner. Treating learners with respect is also important; a hospital which treats its medical students as non-entities and junior staff as 'pairs of hands' will produce poorly motivated doctors who perpetuate those attitudes. It is sometimes feared that learners will become arrogant and overconfident if not kept in their place; I believe that the reverse is true. Brash self-confidence is often a mask covering insecurity. Effective training helps the learner know his strength and limitations and should be done in an environment in which open self-criticism and constructive criticism of others is not hampered by competition and fear of losing face. One of the strengths of training rotations is not just the diversity of clinical exposure but also the range of personalities and attitudes encountered. Trainees are shrewd at noticing differences, strengths, and weaknesses and will take with them the models which fit them best.

## Learning attitudes in specific settings

Attitudinal teaching is not the preserve of any one educational setting. Lectures can be used to convey enthusiasm and establish priorities. Small-group learning allows students to express views and test their own attitudes against those of others. Tutorials allow the teacher to explore and discuss attitudes. Of all settings, the ward round is perhaps best placed to develop attitudes because learning takes place alongside 'live' clinical practice which is, after all, the end-point of training. The patient is present in body as well as spirit and the teacher can give attitudes their due importance both in discussion and, as a role model, in the way he practises his art.

# Role play and video-recorded consultation

Nothing highlights attitudes better than to be on the receiving end of medical care. Role-played consultations allow trainees to develop their consultation skills and receive feedback. They can also put the learner into the patient's shoes when roles are reversed. Learners will not only be sensitive to the performance of their 'doctor' but will feel the influence of his attitudes. Some of the benefit will be subconscious but some will come out in the discussion which follows a role-play exercise or video recording. Role play can be damaging to confidence so it is important to observe the rule of giving positive before negative feedback and commenting on strengths as well as weaknesses. Only a minority of medical trainees have the luxury of video-recording their consultations but, again, this can provide an opportunity to look not just at performance but at the attitudes which underlie it.

# Attitude development programmes

Some curricula, notably that of the University of Maastricht, offer attitude awareness training to medical students or postgraduates. This starts with the premise that appropriate attitudes are fundamental to good clinical practice but are hard to define and even harder to teach. What a curriculum *can* do is help learners understand their own attitudes and how they affect their behaviour. This is done by presenting to a small peer group and tutor a situation which they found challenging. The group analyses the situation, using role play to test alternative strategies for handling it in a way which highlights the impact of attitudes and leaves the learners to reflect on how they might respond to future situations. This is a powerful technique which requires skilled tutoring and a strong mutual sense of responsibility between learners.

# Conclusion

Teachers are asked to teach because they are good at the job which the trainee hopes to learn. Clinical skill is an amalgam of wisdom, skill, and favourable attitudes. I have set out to convey the message that teachers can influence attitudes and encourage self-instruction and personal development but cannot do the learning task for the student. You, like your trainees, have to find your own way of being a more effective teacher. If you feel more enthusiastic and confident in doing so, this chapter has achieved its aim!

**Key points**

- Help learners understand, rather than 'teach'.

- Teach interactively whenever possible.

- Always start by identifying the learners' needs.

- Know your learners and treat them as individuals.

- Clarify the use of language.

- Decide what key points your learners should understand.

- Aim for competence, not abstruse theoretical knowledge.

- Do not forget attitude development; it is central to good clinical practice.

- Favourable attitudes are hard to define but easy to recognize and reinforce.

- Important factors in attitude development are:
  - an open and strong relationship with your learners
  - appraisal
  - role modelling
  - a supportive and well-organized learning environment.

# 4 Teaching manual skills

## Stephen Brearley

Manual skills are an inalienable part of all forms of clinical practice. Included under this heading are not only the techniques of complex surgical operations but also a range of procedures in which all doctors should be competent (venepuncture, the ability to carry out a thorough physical examination, cardiopulmonary resuscitation). Teaching of manual skills begins during basic medical education but constitutes a major part of specialist (postgraduate) training. Manual skills need to be maintained, perfected, and extended throughout a career, however, and should therefore be addressed in continuing medical education (CME).

Motivation to learn manual skills is usually high as technical competence is essential for satisfactory, successful, and fulfilling clinical practice. Lack of confidence in technical ability may be an important cause of stress among junior doctors, which most are keen to overcome by seeking appropriate training as early as possible. Fewer doctors are happy to allow their clinical skills to be subjected to critical scrutiny once they have received such training, but self-assessment of competence can lead to self-delusion. The teaching of manual skills must therefore include monitoring of subsequent performance and constructive feedback from the trainer.

## What should be taught: setting objectives

The full range of skills which a doctor needs will be determined by his or her career goals but a considerable number may be regarded as 'generic', in other words a part of the technical armamentarium of any independently practising doctor. Others are specific to particular specialties, though many of these build upon the generic skills.

There is a degree of logic in the order in which skills should be taught. The experience and dexterity acquired in performing simpler tasks are invaluable when the trainee comes to learn more complex ones, a generalization which holds good at all stages of training, even the most advanced. All of the generic skills, and some of the more advanced ones, can nonetheless be learned within a year or two of graduation and must have been mastered before the doctor is likely to embark on independent practice.

There is no universally accepted list of generic skills but some steps have been taken towards one. In particular, the former British Postgraduate Medical Federation published a logbook for house officers listing a large number of practical procedures which it would be appropriate for newly qualified doctors to be taught (Box 4.1). This list goes beyond the essential and competence in every procedure is not a prerequisite for satisfactory completion of this stage of training, but the existence of such a list is helpful in defining trainees' expectations and trainers' responsibilities.

## Training agreements

There is considerable variation from country to country and specialty to specialty in the extent to which the teaching of manual skills is regulated. Not surprisingly, this tends to be more usual in surgical specialties and, in some European countries, trainee surgeons have to complete a schedule of operations before receiving specialist certification. Such lists of competencies relate to only one aspect of specialist training and should not be seen as defining the point at which a trainee becomes a specialist, but their existence helps in the construction and monitoring of properly structured training programmes.

Even without such official curricula, training is more effective if trainer and trainee agree objectives between themselves at the beginning of their association. Even before this, it is desirable that the training being offered should be spelt out as clearly as possible in advertisements for posts and in trainees' job descriptions. Trainer and trainee should discuss individual needs in the light of this, concentrating on stage in training, achievements to date, perceived strengths and weaknesses, and particular interests or ambitions. This approach is applicable to all aspects of training. It should result in a clear and preferably written statement of objectives as far as training in manual skills is concerned, covering techniques of physical examination, diagnostic procedures, therapeutic manoeuvres, and operative procedures.

In the United Kingdom, formal implementation of these principles has taken place in accordance with the recommendations contained in

**Box 4.1:** Procedures which may be taught to doctors in the first years after qualification (from the BPMF logbook, extensively modified by the author). The essential skills may be regarded as 'generic' to all practising doctors

**Essential**
venepuncture
insertion of i.v. cannula
parenteral drug administration
urinary catheterization
maintenance of airway
emergency ventilation
drain pneumothorax
external cardiac massage
control of external bleeding

**Desirable**
insertion of central venous line
arterial blood sampling
nasogastric intubation
endotracheal intubation
DC cardioversion
pleural aspiration
paracentesis abdominis
proctoscopy
suturing and knotting
excision of skin lesions
drainage of abscesses

**Optional**
insertion of arterial cannula
lumbar puncture
pacing wire insertion
sigmoidoscopy
peritoneal dialysis
liver biopsy
joint aspiration/injection
drainage of hydrocoele

*Training for the Future* (the Calman report). The considerable shortening of the duration of specialist training which this report envisaged demands that training objectives should be more explicit than has been the case previously, and committees of the medical Royal Colleges have published curricula of training for each specialty. Each trainee is party to a 'training agreement', signed also by representatives of the postgraduate dean and the training institution, and each has a personal training plan drawn up jointly with the trainer. These plans detail the skills, as well as the knowledge and experience, which the trainee is expected to acquire during each phase of training, and form the basis of annual reviews of progress.

The detailed specification of training objectives and responsibilities is a logical continuation of developments which were already under way in specialist training and represent a formalization of good practice. It is clearly essential if specialist training is to be completed reliably within a tight timescale, though it leaves unresolved the problem of finding sufficient trainer and trainee time to meet educational obligations.

## Methods of teaching manual skills: general principles

In teaching a manual skill, the trainer must first decide whether this will be best done in a clinical setting, in simulation or, possibly, outside the workplace altogether. These options are discussed below. The teaching may also be given individually or to a small group, and by a variety of teachers. Whatever the setting, a number of general principles apply.

Although opportunities to learn and practise skills may arise unpredictably in clinical work, teaching should, where possible, be planned in advance. Trainers should try to warn trainees beforehand of the intended teaching and may encourage them to do some relevant reading. An attempt should be made to protect the session from interruption by bleeps and other extraneous concerns.

Some consideration may need to be given to the environment in which the teaching is done. Is there sufficient space, privacy, lighting, and ventilation? Are chairs required, and how should they be arranged? What about audio-visual aids? And is all the necessary equipment to hand?

For teaching in simulation, the Royal College of Surgeons of England recommends a four-step procedure. This can be adapted to teaching in the clinical setting, though it may only be possible to cover one or two of the steps on a given occasion. The steps are:

1    instructor demonstrates the task at normal speed, without commentary

2    instructor demonstrates the task slowly, talking through each step

3    learner talks through each step while instructor carries out task

4    learner carries out task, talking through each step.

Although at first sight rather cumbersome, this system works well in practice and has the clear advantage of ensuring that the learner has understood each step of the procedure. It is intended for teaching tasks which take at most five minutes to complete, but many longer procedures, such as surgical operations, can easily be broken down into component parts taking no longer than this.

Teaching of skills should be followed by feedback, which should aim to be positive and constructive. This may be best achieved by asking the trainee what he or she has done well and then what might be improved. Trainers should be aware that trainees may be apprehensive about tackling new skills and that stress may impair performance. A relaxed and encouraging approach is therefore called for.

## Teaching skills in a clinical setting

Although some manual skills can be taught and practised in simulations, none of these reproduces the clinical situation exactly. Participation in clinical work, with delegated responsibility for carrying out practical procedures under appropriate supervision, is therefore a prerequisite for the acquisition of manual skills. Furthermore, while competence in simpler procedures may be attained after only a few repetitions, true dexterity, such as is required for more complex surgical procedures, can only be built up by the regular and prolonged practice which is also characteristic of sportsmen, musicians, and craftsmen. Training centres must recognize this need for extensive practical experience and their ability to provide it should be assessed and monitored by regulatory bodies. Training provided in centres which do not offer adequate practical experience with appropriate teaching and supervision should not be recognized.

Trainers should consider how their clinical work can be planned to maximize training opportunities, for instance by designating a clinic, an operating list, a ward round, or another session as having a major training content and booking patients accordingly. Teaching of the skills of physical examination is particularly liable to be neglected in postgraduate training, but this can be overcome if time is made for trainee and trainer to see patients together, both in the clinic and on the wards.

The general principles set out above should be applied to teaching in the clinical setting. The trainer may find it difficult to resist taking over from a trainee who is clearly finding a task taxing, but this impulse should be resisted unless the patient is in danger of suffering harm as it gives rise to frustration, resentment, and loss of confidence.

Trainers must judge how often an individual trainee needs to be supervised before being allowed to carry out a procedure alone. A gradual reduction in the level of supervision may be appropriate, the trainer being immediately available but not present in the room once a degree of confidence and skill has been achieved. Once satisfied that the trainee is capable of doing a procedure safely, and for appropriate indications, it is perfectly acceptable for him or her to be authorized to do it without supervision.

## Teaching skills in simulation

There is an inevitable 'opportunity cost' inherent in all forms of clinical training, the result of expenditure of the trainer's time and of the extra time which trainees may need to complete unfamiliar tasks. Notwithstanding a degree of artificiality, simulation is a cost-effective way of teaching skills. It also enables the trainee to concentrate on a clearly defined task, avoids the numerous distractions inherent in a clinical situation, allows the trainee to repeat a procedure until it is mastered, and offers the possibility of instantaneous feedback. Trainees who have learned a skill in simulation are likely to feel greater confidence when attempting it for the first time in clinical practice, a confidence which may well be transmitted to the patient.

The 'skills laboratory' was first developed at the University of Limburg in Maastricht and many more have been set up by medical schools and Royal Colleges, equipped with remarkably realistic mannequins and plastic body parts. (These may now be obtained from commercial suppliers.) At about the same time, anastomosis workshops were developed by the Royal College of Surgeons of England, using pig viscera as the raw material, and similar courses are now offered by many hospitals, often with the support of manufacturers. More recently, the College has devised three-day basic surgical skills courses for those in the first year or two of surgical training, teaching suturing and knotting, anastomotic techniques, and basic laparoscopic surgery, all in simulation. It will shortly become mandatory for those entering the College's new MRCS examination to have attended one of these courses, and they are now being run in a number of centres in Britain.

Simulators have long been available for both upper and lower gastrointestinal endoscopy. These are useful not only for teaching basic control and manipulation of the instrument during diagnostic examination but also for practising interventional techniques, such as bile duct cannulation and polypectomy.

Because of the rapid increase in demand for minimally invasive surgery, and the considerable potential for harm through inexpert use of laparoscopic techniques, there has been particular interest in simulation in this area. The Royal College of Surgeons of England has set up a 'Minimal Access Training Unit', headed by a consultant surgeon, to provide suitable courses. In addition to simulations, the unit has video links to operating theatres in a number of hospitals, allowing operations to be viewed live. Other centres with an established reputation in minimally invasive surgery also offer training. Courses usually comprise a theoretical element, video recordings of operations, practice using normal instrumentation on a simulator, and an opportunity to carry out one or more genuine operations under the supervision of an experienced laparoscopic surgeon. Such courses are a good example of the way in which established specialists, many of whom completed their training before the era of laparoscopic surgery, can update and develop their skills.

The scope of simulation may soon expand greatly as a result of computer-generated 'virtual reality'. This is particularly applicable to minimally invasive surgery since both simulated and real operations are viewed on a television monitor. Current prototypes are still relatively crude and enormous computing power will be needed to give anything like a realistic simulation, but enthusiasts for this technology claim that it will be possible in the future to build up anatomically exact models of individual patients from CT or MRI scans, enabling surgeons to practise unique operations before carrying them out in real life.

A spectacular example of successful training using simulation are Advanced Trauma and Cardiac Life Support courses. Although didactic in the extreme, these courses instil a systematic method of managing critically ill patients. The trauma courses employ a manual and lectures but also practical training at eight 'skill stations' and realistic simulations of injured patients ('moulages') using trained volunteers. The skill stations cover airway management, shock, head injury, chest radiology, radiology of the spine, immobilization and extraction, creation of a surgical airway, and chest decompression. They employ mannequins, sophisticated simulators, and sometimes cadavers. The ratio of one instructor to two trainees ensures both close supervision and ample opportunity to practise.

It is feasible for individual trainers to adopt many of these methods for their own use, and many British hospitals already do so in respect of cardiopulmonary resuscitation. Postgraduate medical centres are beginning to develop their own skills laboratories. Trainers should be aware of available courses and should encourage their trainees to make use of them, but they should complement hospital-based training rather than replace it. A considerable number of manual skills are difficult to teach in simulation and extensive clinical experience will remain essential to technical mastery for the foreseeable future.

# Who should teach manual skills?

A great deal of the teaching of manual skills is carried out not by trainers themselves but by trainees who have already mastered those skills, by other senior doctors and, in certain situations, by paramedical staff or nurses. Many hospitals have resuscitation officers, amongst whose responsibilities is the training of junior medical staff. Some of the skills required by junior doctors are rarely used by their seniors and are undoubtedly best taught by those who have an ongoing mastery of them. Recent research suggests that this applies, *inter alia*, to resuscitation skills.

Consultant trainers are not obliged to teach their trainees all the skills they need personally but they are responsible, as educational supervisors, for ensuring that the skills are taught by someone competent to do so. When such delegation takes place, trainers should make sure that both the trainee and the person accepting educational responsibility understand their respective roles. Teaching is in itself a learning experience and should, therefore, be a part of every trainee's job. This applies even to the most junior, who often provide valuable teaching to medical students.

# Assessment and feedback

Regular, critical scrutiny of performance and unambiguous, constructive feedback are essential elements of good educational practice but they have, in the past, been notably absent from many specialist training programmes. Partly, this is because they are time-consuming but there is an inherent reluctance, if not embarrassment, on the part of trainers to engage in it. As a result, educational opportunities are lost. In general, progress towards meeting the training objectives should be formally reviewed halfway through a period of training and again at the end, but more frequent, less formal reviews should occur almost constantly.

It is a peculiarity of medical training that technical competence is rarely subjected to independent, objective assessment by examination or any other means. It is therefore uniquely the role of the trainer to assess it, to ensure that any deficiencies are remedied, and to testify to training bodies and to potential employers that an acceptable standard has been attained. Since there are no agreed criteria of technical sufficiency, this is a subjective matter. Medical audit is rarely able to detect deficiencies because of the crudeness of outcome measures, the numerous other factors which influence outcomes, the poor quality of much audit data, and the small number of cases available for study. The consequences for the trainee of being judged technically deficient are severe, and this may make some trainers reluctant to declare their anxieties.

An accurate assessment by the trainer demands that he or she should observe a reasonable sample of the trainee's work. This may not be easy if work practices and service pressures lead trainers and trainees to work separately for much of the time. Once again, trainers need to consider how they can organize their clinics, operating lists, and ward work so as to ensure adequate contact with their trainees. The need for them to do so must be made clear to service managers.

Just as in the teaching of communication skills, video recordings can be very valuable in teaching manual skills. It is surprising, when this method is so widely used in sports coaching, that video analysis is so unusual in medical training. In the United States, many operations are now video-taped for medico-legal reasons, and the practice is spreading to the UK. The learning of many procedures might be enhanced by video feedback.

Few trainees are so lacking in dexterity that they cannot master the generic manual skills and most are capable of becoming competent surgeons, but occasionally a trainee's performance does give cause for concern. Instinctively, the trainer is likely to blame the trainee's lack of aptitude but other explanations should be considered. These include poor early training, a clash of personalities, valid differences in approach, and personal or psychological problems. The investigation of these possibilities may require considerable sensitivity. In general, the trainer should make his or her concerns known to the trainee as early as possible and seek a joint approach to solving the problem. Health services are not usually well adapted to providing remedial training in any field but an effort should be made to correct any identifiable shortcomings in early training. No trainee's career should be terminated on the advice of a single trainer and any trainee in difficulties should have an opportunity of working with, and being assessed by, another trainer.

## Maintenance of manual skills

Manual skills, once learned, are probably never forgotten, but maintaining a satisfactory standard requires regular practice. Doctors practising independently have a responsibility to ensure that they do maintain the skills which they require in their field of work in good order, and should consider limiting their practice if they feel unable to do so.

There are at present no 'recertification' procedures for doctors in any European country, either at basic or specialist level, though recertification based upon regular participation in continuing medical education has existed in the United States for a considerable time. In the United Kingdom, the General Medical Council has introduced procedures for dealing with doctors whose professional performance is consistently poor and several of the medical Royal Colleges are becoming interested in the reaccreditation of specialists. All require their members and fellows to submit details of their participation in CME. The issue is also under discussion in the Advisory Committee on Medical Training of the European Union.

Workshops and courses designed to teach new skills to established doctors, or to refresh old ones, have become more numerous, however, and participation in them is encouraged. The same courses may indeed serve both to teach trainees and to update their seniors. All doctors should be competent in cardiopulmonary resuscitation and it would not be unreasonable for employers to insist on regular training in this for all staff. Verifiable levels of skill in other defined areas may similarly become mandatory for certain groups of doctors. Participation in medical audit also plays a role in maintaining levels of skill, though its shortcomings are well recognized.

The rate of advancement of medical knowledge is so rapid that no doctor can expect to enter independent practice with a range of skills sufficient to last a professional lifetime. Regular reskilling of the medical workforce will become ever more necessary in the future and all those involved in medical education need to make provision for this.

### Key points

- A four-step approach to teaching manual skills is recommended: instructor demonstrates; instructor demonstrates the task slowly with commentary; learner describes each step as instructor carries out the task; learner carries out task, commenting on each step.

- Gradual reduction in supervision is possible if a skill has been mastered.

- Accurate assessment of manual skills requires the trainer to observe the trainee's work.

- Video-recording can be a valuable means for teaching manual as well as communication skills.

# 5 Supervision and mentoring

*Trevor Bayley*

Senior doctors are often asked to become a supervisor without having any previous experience or training. For some, this brings anxiety because of uncertainty about what the process entails. For others, becoming a supervisor is part of a natural progression, from trainee to trainer, and transition is smooth.

## The qualities of a supervisor

Few possess all the attributes of an 'ideal' supervisor; and the 'ideal' supervisor for one trainee may not be the best for another. The qualities needed in a supervisor include empathy, understanding, genuineness, concern, attentiveness, and openness. The importance of each of these qualities varies according to the trainee and his/her level of training as well as the setting where supervision occurs (clinic, ward, operating theatre, community, etc.). In performance of the role, a supervisor has also to be able to consider different perspectives: that of the trainee; that of the other members of the team, including other trainees; and that of the patient.

Supervisors may also have sub-roles as teacher, assessor, counsellor, colleague, 'boss', and expert. Achieving the best blend of these in supervision of a particular trainee varies between specialties, and requires both conscious effort and experience in handling the authority and power inherent in the role. The supervisor needs to avoid a threatening approach and, equally, one which is patronizing in order to teach without showing off knowledge and to gain the trust of the supervisee, both as a confidante and a practitioner.

# The process of supervision

Supervision involves an interpersonal, one-to-one relationship which facilitates the professional development and competence of the supervisee. The task of supervision has three main functions: educative, supportive, and managerial. Which is the most important of these three functions will vary according to the setting, the specialty, and the level of the trainee. Although the educative or formative aspects are of prime importance in describing the functions of an educational supervisor, the same person (the trainee's consultant, for example) may also have managerial responsibility for the supervisee. Although it is arguably better for the supervisor to fulfil only one of these three functions, this is not always possible in small units. When the supervisor has to perform all three functions it is important to achieve a proper balance for successful supervision, and that the supervisee knows, at any one time, the mode which the supervisor is adopting.

# Educational supervision

If educational supervision is the principal function, the supervisor should be concerned with:

- the content and process of the supervisee's training
- ensuring that there is ample time in which the trainee can reflect on these aspects of learning.

The supervisor, in an educational role, is concerned with the development of a trainee's understanding and personal or technical skills. Additionally, he or she has responsibility for ensuring a trainee develops an ability to learn through work, from tasks performed, and through fulfilling a service need. Probably most importantly, he should provide faithful and prompt feedback on performance. Feedback allows the supervisor to assess the trainee's educational needs and to advise on how deficiencies might be overcome.

Supervisors having an educative function often provide some personal support for their supervisee as well. Support for the supervisee should ensure that, according to his training level, he neither has unnecessarily difficult tasks to perform nor very complex problems to solve. Support also allows the supervisee to know that he can expect and receive opportunities to discuss problems, and that the supervisor understands how these could affect a trainee's work and ability to learn. In this pastoral role the supervisor should be able to recognize any features of stress, and the apathy and loss of interest in learning which may be indicators of so-called 'burn out'.

Even though he may not be the line manager for a trainee, the educational supervisor needs to ensure that the work and tasks of the trainee are appropriate to his abilities and that these utilize his skills properly. For example, demeaning tasks both destroy a trainee's motivation to learn and result in loss of confidence in the supervisor as an advocate for his training.

## A supervisory contract

A contract or agreement between the supervisor and trainee is valuable in defining a clear and enabling relationship. The categories or levels of supervision to be provided should be agreed and understood. This is particularly important in technical specialties and in some aspects of psychiatry training. Such an agreement, indicating the level of educative supervision to be provided and expected, also allows the responsibilities for non-educational, managerial supervision to be clearly understood. The contract enables supervisor and supervisee to understand 'boundaries', i.e. what aspects of the latter's work are being supervised and what are not. An educational contract will, ideally, gain the trainee's trust in the confidentiality of the supervisor/supervisee relationship. A description of mutual expectations should assist the development of that relationship.

## Supervisory style

There are many supervisory styles; one or more may be the most appropriate for a certain specialty. Some medical teachers favour a non-directive, supervisee-centred approach; however, the style needed will vary according to circumstances, including the setting, the personality of the supervisor, and that of the trainee. It is important for the supervisor to recognize how his or her background and attitudes affect style, particularly if these differ from those of the supervisee. The style needed and employed is also likely to vary with the professional development of the trainee, and supervisors should, ideally, be able to alter their style accordingly. Those who select supervisors must be aware of the individual's style and how this is likely to match the needs of a particular trainee.

## Development of the supervisee

Supervisee development should be described according to stages. This approach is helpful both in assessing progress and in providing information to another supervisor when the supervisee moves to another setting or attachment. The developmental stages through which a supervisee passes are, in many ways, similar to those of an apprentice learning a craft:

- level one – the most junior trainee, equivalent to the novice (a preregistration officer)

- level two – a journeyman (typically, a senior house officer)

- level three – a largely independent craftsman (an experienced registrar)

- level four – finally, the master craftsman (the certificated trainee, ready for fully independent practice).

A level one trainee is characteristically dependent on the supervisor. The trainee is often anxious, has difficulty in assessing his or her own performance, together with an accompanying feeling of insecurity. At this stage the trainee requires a structured teaching programme, with a didactic teaching style when the trainee is learning practical skills. Unambiguous and explicit feedback on performance and attitudes is essential at this level.

At level two, the trainee, having overcome most of his initial anxieties, can show fluctuation between continuing dependence on the supervisor and autonomy. Some liken this to the problems faced by the parent of an adolescent. Some containment is necessary for patient safety, whilst allowing the trainee to learn from the experience of making mistakes. The teaching programme at this stage may be less structured, although content is important, and should not be as didactic as that provided for trainees at level one.

By level three the trainee has already acquired a degree of professional self-confidence, with only rare need to depend on the supervisor. At this stage the trainee is able to understand the practice of his specialty in a wider context. He shows an ability to adapt, and supervision becomes a matter of sharing experience – but with occasional confrontation if there is disagreement about clinical management.

Finally, at level four, the trainee has 'insightful awareness' and knows how to confront professional problems. By this stage the trainee is ready to become a supervisor as well, having achieved mastery of the specialty.

At this stage there is less need for further knowledge but more for deeper understanding and integration.

## Group supervision

Economies of time and availability of expertise may result in group rather than individual supervision. Group supervision has an important advantage: it provides the support of peers who are also involved in the same process, i.e. the sharing of experiences and feedback with others. It also has disadvantages: there is less time for each person to receive supervision; and the process can, for some, be destructive and undermining, particularly if there is competition between members. It is clearly important to select membership of the group with care. Those who feel unable to discuss their performance openly are unsuited to group supervision.

## Mentoring

Mentoring differs from supervision principally in its aims and in the relationship between mentor and trainee. The aim of mentoring is to both help and facilitate the individual in achieving his or her full career potential. The mentor is managerially more experienced than the subject and is chosen because it is perceived he is likely to be able to pass on his wisdom and use his expertise to achieve these aims. It is probably best for mentors to be selected by those who are to be mentored. The relationship between mentor and trainee has to be negotiated and may not always be ideal. It may be necessary to change mentors – this is not necessarily a sign of failure of the process but may be an indication that the relationship is mature and allows the individuals to acknowledge that change will be beneficial. Mentoring may be a prolonged relationship, lasting for several years or for a limited period, say, one year.

## The process of mentoring

The basis of mentoring is the definition of learning and development objectives. Those objectives need to be attainable and measurable; both mentor and subject must agree on what is to be accomplished and draw up a plan with realistic timescales. This forms a 'learning contract' between the two. The process of mentoring also involves a review of those objectives.

The mentor has other functions which provide direct assistance with the trainee's career and professional development:

- giving advice and guidance on career and professional development
- acting as a sponsor and advocate
- possibly (but not necessarily) training and instructing the trainee
- providing information on learning and career opportunities
- arranging appropriate professional experience in the broad sense
- providing clarification on goals and professional values
- stimulating acquisition of knowledge
- acting as a role model.

Mentors may also provide emotional and psychological support, providing encouragement and accepting the responsibility involved. The mentor is not usually involved in assessment of the trainee; the supervisor, who does not have responsibility for providing emotional and psychological support, fulfils this function.

Mentors may be responsible for providing guidance to those in training and established, senior doctors, although their functions for a trainee will clearly differ from those for a senior colleague. The mentor of a senior doctor must command respect and have the confidence of that person. The same applies to the mentor of a doctor in training, but their relationship is more akin to that of teacher/pupil.

## Mentors

The mentor may be a more senior and experienced colleague; alternatively, the mentor may be a peer (particularly when the trainee is also a senior doctor). The peer mentor need not be working in the same specialty, although he should be able to help the trainee to reflect on practice.

Mentors should be senior doctors with understanding and experience of the working system. To be effective, a mentor should inspire trust and possess good interpersonal skills. Willingness to help and an interest in doing so are necessary. Honesty is also essential. Other desirable attributes include:

- empathy towards the problems of the trainee

- frankness in discussing professional development
- confidentiality
- a non-judgemental approach to the task.

Mentors must be aware of the danger of encouraging a belief in their omniscience: a so-called 'halo' effect. The trainee is likely to be overawed by a mentor unless it is clear that he too is fallible. Helping a subject to understand poor performance is an important – and possibly the most difficult – function of the peer mentor. The mentor works through encouragement of the trainee to identify their strengths and weaknesses, but can only do this if he is trusted and known to be honest. Peer mentoring should ideally encourage self-assessment and from this identify learning activities.

## The benefits of mentoring

Mentors for both those in training and senior doctors should help their protégés to develop new insights into their practice and learning needs as well as a fresh perspective on their training or continuing professional development. They may act as a catalyst in the development of new approaches to clinical practice and to consideration of further training. The mentor encourages self-analysis through reflection on practice and professional development, and by this facilitates change. The continuing education and professional development of senior doctors requires an assessment of need. Mentors can facilitate this process by helping their subjects to identify learning activities, how these might be attained, and what outcomes should result.

---

**Key points**

- Supervision has three main functions: educative, supportive, and managerial.

- Educational supervision is concerned with the content and process of training and provision of time for reflection on learning.

- Educational contracts describe mutual expectations of the supervisor and supervisee.

- Supervisory style should match the needs of the supervised.

- The stage of development of the supervisee should be assessed when deciding the supervisor.

- Group supervision has the advantage of peer support but membership requires careful selection.

- Mentors should be selected and not imposed.

- The basis of mentoring is the definition of learning and development objectives.

- A mentor should inspire trust and be honest.

- A mentor has an educative, professional development and personal counselling role.

# 6 Teaching communication

## Carl Whitehouse

In recent years teaching communication has become a key element in medical education. One reason for this is that doctors have learnt that deficiency in communication leads to errors in diagnosis, inappropriate use of resources, and poor compliance with treatment.

Meanwhile, patients rightly want to share in understanding what is happening to them when they are ill and to participate in decisions about their care. Poor communication leads to dissatisfaction.

Emphasis on the need for good communication means that these skills feature increasingly in both undergraduate and postgraduate assessments. This motivates students at all levels to seek help to develop their abilities in the field.

## Does communication need to be taught?

In the past, the main emphasis was on the elicitation of information from the patient. This was a one-way and highly focused transaction. It included learning a range of questions that were intended to cover all the important areas: the history of the presenting complaint, the systems review, the family and social history and the past medical history. Eliciting answers was not thought to depend on learning how to relate to patients: this was considered a natural ability.

In recent years there has been a shift to a wider focus which includes elucidation as well as elicitation of the patient's symptoms. This requires clarification of the information they provide. The wider focus also extends to providing information for patients and negotiating decisions with them. All these require specific skills to be built on to the natural social aptitudes. These skills have to be taught.

It has also become evident that even natural aptitudes and attitudes are sometimes deficient. Even when present, they can regress if not reinforced, so that it is possible for students and young doctors to become worse at relating to patients. It has been demonstrated, for instance, that first-year students are less likely to avoid emotionally difficult topics and more likely to enquire about the patient's own views of their problem than final-year students. There is plenty of evidence of the lack of appropriate skills amongst qualified doctors in both hospital and general practice.

## What needs to be learned

An effective doctor needs to acquire abilities to communicate in a whole range of situations. The most obvious situation is communication between doctor and patient, but even here different approaches are required. First, the doctor must have learnt to make contact with a patient, building trust and confidence so that the patient feels able to share the problem with the doctor.

Second, the doctor must be able to listen effectively to what the patient wants to share.

Third, the doctor must be able to take a history of the patient's problems in such a way as to elicit and elucidate the information needed to make a rational definition of those problems.

Fourth, the doctor must be able to share an understanding of the problem with the patient. The doctor must be able to explain the nature of the problem in language the patient can comprehend and also explain management options in such a way that the patient can make a valid decision about treatment.

Sometimes the problem will be serious so that any explanation counts as 'bad news'. Fifth, then, the doctor needs to be able to break bad news in a way that shows care and concern for the patient.

In covering these five areas, doctors have to learn to cope with a number of difficulties:

- they must be able to communicate with people with limited linguistic skills, especially those for whom English is a second language

- they must understand how factors such as age, gender, social class, and culture can affect communication, and be able to respond to this

- they must be able to cope with situations where communication is impaired. Such impairment may be due to age (the very young or very old), physical disability, or mental disability. Physical disability may impair communication in a range of ways, from deafness or blindness to such emotional consequences of illness as pain, fear, anger, or denial. Mental causes of impairment can similarly range from brain damage or mental illness, through the effects of alcohol or drugs, to learning disabilities.

In facing these different issues, doctors are not automata. The questions they have to ask and the responses they get often engage their own emotions:

- they therefore must be able to cope with embarrassment, particularly in talking about areas that are outside normal social conversation: questions relating to sexuality and various bodily functions
- they must also be able to cope with their own reactions to patient emotions such as anger, tearfulness, withdrawing, and denial.

The second situation doctors meet is the need to communicate with relatives and carers. First, there are many issues in this situation similar to those experienced with patients. Doctors must be able to explain medical issues in a language that the hearer understands, whilst responding to the concerns expressed by the hearer. Doctors must be able to cope with gaps of age, gender, culture, and social class. Doctors must be able to cope when communication is impaired, especially by the emotional responses of relatives when faced with bad news.

Second, doctors must be able to interpret and allow for bias when they receive information from close relatives. Doctors must understand the factors that affect a relative's view, from the anxiety of a young mother to the frustration of an elderly carer.

Third, doctors must be aware of the ethics of confidentiality. A doctor needs to know who has a right to any information they possess. Even saying nothing can be misinterpreted and lead to unnecessary distress and suffering, so doctors also need to develop a range of skills in sensitive discussion.

The final situation doctors find themselves in is the need to communicate with other health professionals. This includes other doctors and many other members of the caring team. There are two new areas here: much of the communication is written as well as verbal and much of the interaction occurs within groups. Doctors must:

- be able to summarize information and plans on paper
- be able to write succinct but accurate reports and referral requests

- have dictating skills to enable them to make effective use of secretarial support

- be able to use telephone and electronic communication systems

- be able to participate in a group, or team, both listening and contributing effectively. This may require some skills in asserting themselves.

The undergraduate student therefore has a wide range of learning needs in the field of communication in order to become an effective doctor. This range of needs will continue to need to be addressed in postgraduate training. Understanding this range enables us to set our aims as teachers.

---

**Key points**

Doctors need to learn how to communicate with patients, with carers, and with other team members. This requires a number of competencies ranging from building trust to listening and sharing. It requires that they can cope with their own emotions as well as those of those they seek to help. It requires an understanding of the ethics of confidentiality and yet the importance of sharing information within teams.

---

# The aims of teaching communication

Our broad aim should be to enable students at whatever level to communicate with patients, carers, and colleagues in such a way that they can work with them to provide effective, safe, and humane medical care. To do this requires the development of knowledge, skills, and attitudes.

## Knowledge

Providing a knowledge base is important in securing understanding and motivation. We constantly come up against the concepts that 'communication is natural' and what we are teaching is common sense. Whilst there is a grain of truth in such assertions, understanding is required of the evidence for the need to learn communication skills and also of the theoretical underpinning of some of the approaches used. A number of instances can focus our teaching aims:

- there is evidence that when doctors and patients do not agree on the nature of the problem the patient is unlikely to be committed to the management suggested by the doctor. This leads to what doctors call 'non-compliance', especially with ambulant patients in the community who can decide whether to take the medication or attend the treatment centre. It also leads to dissatisfaction, even for recumbent patients in hospital who do not understand the treatment plan they are subjected to. An understanding of this evidence and its implications helps in the recognition of such disagreements and in considering how to negotiate to gain agreement

- there is evidence that failure of communication leads to difficulty in determining the real problem of a patient. This evidence also shows how the use of certain skills, such as deploying open questions, listening to patient responses, and then clarifying particular areas, can improve problem solving. An awareness of this evidence helps to develop appropriate skills in elucidation

- there is evidence that understanding cultural aspects, including differences in communication style, can be helpful, as long as it does not lead to stereotyping of people. In early medical training, students often receive input from behavioural sciences such as psychology, sociology, social anthropology, and even linguistics. We need to learn how to employ the insights gained from these disciplines when dealing with real people

- there is evidence that certain methods of teaching communication, such as audio and video feedback, improve both specific behaviours and the ability to elicit information. An awareness of the value of such approaches helps to prepare people to subject themselves to a threatening situation.

## Skills

The knowledge base provides a background to our intervention, and helps teachers and learners decide which skills we need to acquire to enhance communication, as the evidence above shows.

There are a whole range of skills that we could aim to develop. One list includes the following: making contact, putting people at ease, eliciting information, listening, clarifying, reflecting, use of body posture, facilitating patient expression, sharing information, speaking a common language for the purpose in hand, negotiating, and ending a consultation.

It has become clear that there is a wide range of areas of communication to consider and a variety of skills that might be helpfully developed. It is neither possible, nor usually necessary, to cover everything. To a large extent the right pattern of skills depends on the individual personal style of the learner and, except in extreme instances, it would be wrong to attempt some kind of total social skills retraining. It is preferable to utilize and develop the personal strengths and skills a learner has. In considering aims for learning communication skills, there is a need for individual tailoring.

## Attitudes

It is well recognized that behaviour, whilst related to basic knowledge and appropriate skills, depends on attitudes. Attitudinal development is therefore a main requirement in ensuring good communication. We might say that effective communication means the patient gets what the patient needs, but this begs the question of what the patient does need. If a patient says they want a sleeping tablet, we may be able to argue that they do not need it; if they say they want relief from an intolerable discomfort, that is a need we cannot dispute although we may have different ways of responding to it. We can only ensure an effective response to these deeper needs of a patient if we have empathy with them. Empathy is the ability to be sensitive to another's current feelings and the facility to communicate this understanding in a 'language' attuned to those feelings. Learning communication therefore requires learning to be 'tuned in' and sensitive to individual patients.

But the required attitudes go further than being 'tuned in' to feelings. The doctor must be able to respond to those feelings even when under pressure. This responsiveness is a key element in developing trust and confidence, which is essential if patients are to share their pains and problems and give us insight into their real needs. This trust will also help the doctor to negotiate a plan that will use medical knowledge and skills to deal effectively with those needs. This responsiveness, or patient orientation, means genuinely putting the patient and the patient's views at the centre of the interaction. It is more than demonstrating respect, listening, and exploring and assessing their attitudes and assumptions: it is a genuine and sometimes costly interest and preparedness to act. Learning communication means learning to respond in a patient-centred way.

Perhaps the underlying attitude required is that the doctor or student must believe that the patient has worth. This will lead to a desire to empower and strengthen that patient, even at a cost to themselves. This is difficult, especially if the doctor or student does not immediately like the patient or is prejudiced. It is also difficult if they are under pressure, having to deal with a number of serious situations at the same time. Indeed, the empathic, responsive, patient-centred doctor can appear a paragon of virtue which most of us cannot hope to emulate. Because of the difficulties, there is a tendency to play safe by simply asking the right questions in the right way and using various other techniques to speed up the contact. This is one reason why patient-centredness constantly suffers attrition and requires reinforcement. Learning communication means learning the worth of our patients and also learning self-awareness and an honest appraisal of our strengths, weaknesses, and prejudices.

---

**Key points**

The aims of education in the field of communication can be divided into knowledge, skills, and attitudes. An understanding of the knowledge base helps students perceive the need for time and effort in this field. Specific skills can be taught but are only likely to be used appropriately if students have attitudes of patient-centredness and self-awareness.

---

## Ways and means of teaching communication

In recent years the teaching of communication has been extensively developed in general practice and the undergraduate field. As education develops amongst hospital doctors to reinforce and extend communication skills, the same approaches, based on the same educational principles, are being used. The undergraduate may need more formal input to provide the background knowledge, and will be strongly influenced by the examples demonstrated. Postgraduates will continue to be influenced by the examples around but should be better placed to participate in group work, working from their own experience and learning with peers. Unfortunately, lack of past experience may limit involvement, particularly in techniques such as role play. The value of the similar approaches across the range of educational need should be borne in mind as different techniques are discussed.

## Teaching methods: the skills we demonstrate

Some specific teaching of communication will involve special methods which have an important place in social skills training. However, the majority of learning will come from example rather than precept, and there is no better way to reinforce patient-centredness than providing a good role model and demonstrating how it leads to effective communication at all levels.

As we demonstrate our competence as clinicians we must make sure that we demonstrate our communication skills. Junior colleagues and students will make better use of this modelling if we are also able to highlight from time to time how we employ these skills.

## Putting patients at ease

Teachers should consider how they put patients at ease: what techniques do they use in greeting patients, what names do they use, do they shake hands (or rub noses!), what are their first words, and what position do they assume when starting the consultation. All these things are being watched by those learning.

At the same time students will have individual styles, and there will be areas they need to discuss. They may want to explore the correct style of address. Gone are the days of the patronizing 'Gran', or the universal formal Mr Doe and Mrs Roe, but do all patients like to be called Jack or Jill or...? They may want to explore how we put ourselves on the same physical level as the patient, so that we are not overpowering them.

## Question framing

Having greeted the patient, teachers should consider how they frame questions to gather information. Undergraduate students, in particular, tend to move quickly to closed questions (that can only be answered by yes, or no, or a number) and they need to see how open questions allow the patient to do the talking and really tell the doctor what is wrong. When first learning to take a history, undergraduates can also have difficulty in fitting in the good communication approach (open questions and listening to the patient response) to the need to structure the information so that they get all that is required for the formal history. A structured format is useful to students (and to doctors) because it enables them to review whether they have collected all the relevant data, but it can inhibit the flow of the conversation. If students are taught that they must complete the check-list of questions, they can find it hard to revert to a more open approach, even as their confidence increases. Again there is need for demonstration of how the skilled, experienced doctor communicates. The process is to allow the patient to talk at length, to fill the information in to the internalized structure or check-list, and then to put in some supplementary questions that fill in the gaps that are left: 'You didn't mention whether the pain was there all the time' or 'Did you say you smoked?'.

As question framing is demonstrated, a number of issues may be highlighted:

- students may be shown how a supplementary question was used to clarify information given and to ensure that the doctor fully understood the patient

- students may be shown how a doctor summarized the information and fed it back to the patient to make sure the patient had said all they wanted on the topic

- students may be shown how reflection of a question was used to help elucidate what the patient was saying

- students may also see how we tried to bring out a patient's ideas, concerns, and expectations, and how difficult it can be when patients are ashamed of their (very real) fears.

The more we tune in to our own consultations, the more we will be aware of how we use (or fail to use) these skills, be able to highlight them, and also be able to recognize them in the student's behaviour.

## Listening

It is essential to demonstrate the skills of listening. Neither doctors nor medical teachers are good at this. We tend to dislike silence and interrupt patients or students if they do not respond quickly to a question. This is a specific area where we need to demonstrate in our clinical interaction, and also mirror in our teaching, the skill we want our students to achieve in their interaction with patients. Silence, an attentive and concerned posture, eye contact, and those little verbal encouragements (often called facilitatory grunts) are very easily missed and yet may well be the most important tools in our communication armoury.

## Verbal and non-verbal behaviour

At the same time as body language, sounds, and the occasional respon-sive 'Yes, go on' to encourage the patient to talk, so the doctor needs to watch out for cues provided by the patient. The hesitation, the word that is almost swallowed, the mention of the family or the symptom that seems unconnected and unimportant can all help the doctor to open up the discussion. The position in the chair, the use of a bag or folded arms to protect themselves, the tear-stained face, and other non-verbal aspects are also clues to be used. The teacher must constantly be aware of using such cues and be prepared to highlight them. We easily assume that we all share the same conversational skills and all naturally take these things on board, and act on them. It is evident that this is a false assumption, and people can improve their techniques in this field by increased alertness. Students need to be made aware of things that we may do skilfully but unwittingly.

## Speaking a common language for purpose in hand

The words that we use, particularly when seeking to explain things to a patient, are very important. Again we need to listen to ourselves and ask whether someone who had never done A level Biology would understand what we were talking about.

Undergraduates have a particular tendency to launch into biochemical tutorials, and they need to see how negotiating with a patient means using words and ideas that are mutually understood. This may also require highlighting the different constructs that people put on words. Ulcer and virus are words used in both medical and non-medical circles, but may bring very different ideas to mind.

## Awareness of defence mechanisms

Finally, we need to demonstrate our awareness of defence mechanisms that patients use to overcome their fears and emotional distress. Patients may show denial; they may cover up with a superficial jollity; they may be brusque, irritable, or overtly angry. Students need to be made aware of the emotional complexity of some interactions they watch; they need to see the strategies we employ to deal with different reactions and they need to understand the attitude which enables us to accept much socially inappropriate behaviour.

# Teaching methods: focusing students

While most learning of communication will be by example and role modelling, there is a need for some specific, focused teaching for two reasons. Firstly, it provides a theoretical base which helps students to recognize, understand, and evaluate good communication when they see it. Secondly, it provides a safe space for them to consider bad examples and role models to which, unfortunately and inevitably, they will be exposed and to help them cope with such upsetting experiences.

A number of methods can be used for this more formal input. We can consider them in ascending order of cost, sophistication, and effectiveness.

## Lecture

Lectures are not an ideal format for teaching about communication but they can provide information about the knowledge base. They can also be used to highlight many of the issues demonstrated in other formats.

Lectures can be illustrated in various ways. Videos can be made to demonstrate effective and ineffective communication and to show particular barriers. They can show how simple changes in the structure of the consulting room or the wording of questions can change the whole pattern of a consultation, and can illustrate the effect of body language, non-verbal cues, and question framing.

However, there are certain aspects of the use of video recordings to consider. With commercial videos copyright laws must be observed. Also, we may be tempted sometimes to use a significant example of a communication issue on a video recording that we have taken of our own consultation with real patients for our own education. Here we must be careful about patient confidentiality and be sure that they have given informed consent to the 'public' showing of the consultation in a lecture theatre.

An alternative to video recordings is the use of actors to simulate consultations within the lecture theatre. This can provide a flexible teaching aid.

Actors can be used to highlight the barriers to a consultation in the same way as a film, but with the added advantage of some feedback from the 'doctor' and 'patient' afterwards. Actors can also demonstrate how consultations with different health professionals often leads to different issues being addressed. Consider what happens when a patient with a breast lump sees their general practitioner, a consultant surgeon, and then a breast care nurse: for each consultation the patient will have a different agenda. The fact that the patient does not allow the surgeon to explore the emotional issues fully is not necessarily a reflection on the effectiveness of the surgeon's communication. An actor as a patient can allow a demonstration of all three interactions during one teaching session.

Actors can also take the part of students as well as patients to show some of the difficulties that may arise in a less threatening situation.

Demonstrations of this nature can be used as triggers for group discussion. They should raise issues for students, especially if related to relevant experience either in the day-to-day work or special communication skills sessions.

## Working together: discussion groups

Although lecture formats can raise issues for students, they also need to discuss these issues, to practise their own approaches, and to receive feedback if they are to develop effective communication. Formal communication skills teaching therefore requires much group work.

Within the group it is also possible to look at other interactions, such as those that take place in a team, and this can help in developing some of the wider communication needs.

The simplest group work will be discussion groups in which the students can explore issues that have been raised in other situations such as lectures or their work on the ward. This is valuable in allowing evaluation of role models, in dealing with difficulties and upsets that have arisen, and in focusing on some attitudinal aspects.

As in all group work, the setting and size of the group is important. Discussing social skills is a threatening situation, and the same applies to evaluating the social skills of role models (especially senior and highly respected clinicians). Reasonably uninhibited discussion is difficult with groups of over eight to ten, and is also affected by a ring of uncomfortable chairs in a bare seminar room.

## Working together: task groups

An important use of groups is to analyse actual consultations, especially those carried out by the learners. Sometimes group members may bring recordings carried out in clinical settings, and this is particularly used in postgraduate education. At the undergraduate level the consultations are more commonly arranged especially for the teaching session, using real patients, simulated patients, or role play.

Although it is possible to 'fishbowl' the consultation with the group in the same room as the consultation, video equipment makes a tremendous difference as the students involved in the consultation are much less aware of the observers (and their occasional suppressed expressions of amusement or surprise). If video equipment is used, however, it needs to be of high quality and set up and tested well before the arrival of the group. Difficulty in hearing upsets the group participation whilst technical hitches only increase the tension within the group.

It is helpful if the setting in which the consultation takes place is clinically appropriate. A properly placed desk and chairs, records, and even equipment (even if it is not going to be used) brings a sense of realism which can help the process. At the same time it is important to keep the group work informal – a small room, a circle of the same type of chair, and breaks for refreshment together (with the teachers) all help.

Group size is important, as all individuals should have the opportunity to be actively involved in a consultation. In a session of two to three hours it is unlikely that more than five students can participate effectively.

Although it is quite possible for a single tutor to run the group, it is sometimes useful to have a co-tutor and some units like to share the teaching between a clinician and a behavioural scientist. Simulated patients, discussed below, may also participate as lay co-tutors.

At least one tutor needs to be aware of how to make best use of the video recorder to recall key moments in the tape. Although very valuable on a one-to-one exercise, it is seldom worth going through the video record of a whole consultation with a group, and so this tutor must be adept at noting the tape counter and using the rewind and fast forward buttons.

The main negative factor in running such group task work is the apprehension of the students. Once this is overcome, most students find it very helpful. There are various ways to approach this problem. First, it is important to start from the learners' own needs. Most students can state what they find difficult in communication: it may be the patient who 'won't stop talking and let you get on with your history', or 'deaf patients'. Frequently, undergraduates have questions about 'not knowing what to say'. The tutor can show how these different areas will be addressed over a period of time.

Second, the strengths of students should be recognized. They need to know that they are being asked to develop their own strengths and social skills and to adapt them to the needs of the clinical situation. This is where the use of a positive feedback loop is required. Rules for feedback in analysing general practice consultations have been suggested. These are:

- briefly clarify matters of fact
- the doctor in question goes first
- good points first
- recommendations not criticisms.

A useful modification, especially for undergraduate sessions, is as follows:

- clarify any points of fact
- the learner (i.e. the student who carries out the consultation) states what went well
- the observers state what went well
- the learner states what could have been done differently
- the observers state what might have been done differently
- the learner states what has been learnt.

The importance of these 'rules' is that the emphasis is on the strengths of the learner. When things that might have been done differently are discussed, it is not done with negative, critical connotations but rather as a search for different approaches which might achieve similar ends, and an evaluation of which approach is most applicable to the individual.

Thirdly, it is important to start from simple problems and to move towards the more complex or emotionally charged. This enables students to build confidence before they face difficulties. Students often express concern about having to cope with a tearful patient or having to respond to a question about having cancer early in their contact with real patients. Such concerns do need to be addressed and students need to know they will get help and support when needed, but in reality few students actually face these difficulties. It is important to concentrate on their ability to cope with simpler issues first and build up towards addressing these difficulties.

Task groups can be instrumental in focusing on specific areas of communication, and the consultations can take a number of forms.

## Real patients

A central core of practical experience is received by students and doctors talking to real patients in wards or consulting rooms. At undergraduate level, students enjoy these opportunities but they do not usually provide effective situations for learning communication. There are a number of negative factors:

- students usually talk to patients on their own, so that there is no feedback on how they have performed

- students may be asked to elicit a history in front of a group during a ward round. When this happens there is often a considerable amount of interruption so that they are unable to develop their own style and approach

- the focus is commonly on the information elicited rather than the way it was elicited: for instance the objective of the session may be to learn about asthma rather than learn how to communicate with a patient who complains of being short of breath

- patients have often recounted their problem a number of times and therefore give a patterned response rather than a natural reply to the student's questions. They will even answer questions that have not been asked

- students can be sensitive about exploring areas that they find embarrassing or difficult, especially if they have had no experience

- inexperienced students, and tutors, can be rightly inhibited about discussing and negotiating management plans.

There are a number of ways in which these problems can be overcome, short of video-taping real consultations with group (or one-to-one) feedback afterwards:

- teachers should be clear about their objectives for a particular teaching opportunity. If the aim is to examine consultation skills then the student should be allowed to talk to the patient in as natural a way as possible. If the group is observing, it should seek to fade into the background and not interrupt. The use of a side room makes such a fishbowl approach easier

- once students have some idea of the skills they need to explore and have mastered the basic rules of feedback, it is possible for two students to see a patient together and to provide some feedback to each other

- students can take a small audio cassette to the interview and request permission to tape it. The audio cassette can be reviewed by the student alone, with peers, or with the tutor

- if the patient has discussed their problems a number of times the opportunity can be taken to explore issues other than eliciting basic information. It is particularly valuable to consider the extent to which their ideas have been taken into account and their expectations met

- real patients can be used in group task work but, again, the situation is unnatural for the patient is not consulting a real doctor and often reacts in a different way. Patients often provide students with a life history rather than the responses they would give in a clinical interview. This can be used to explore their perceptions and priorities but it does not provide real consulting experience. If real patients do not necessarily provide such experience, then we need to use other approaches.

## Simulated patients

People with drama skills are increasingly being used as an adjunct in communication skills teaching. Some such actors are volunteers who do little more than role play a set scenario in a repetitive way, and so provide a 'standardized' patient. Other actors, or 'simulators', are highly experienced and able to adapt roles and situations to different needs. These simulators may also continue in role after the initial consultation and provide feedback from within the patient situation. It is also possible for students to try alternative approaches as the simulator can flash back to a key moment in the interview and start again, with the same or a different student, in a highly realistic way. Finally, their experienced but lay background enables them to teach the students from a lay perspective and take a place as full members of the teaching team.

Simulated patients have a major role in enhancing understanding of the patient perspective, and thus promoting attitudinal development. They are also particularly effective in looking at management issues, especially as the student cannot harm the 'patient' if they take an inappropriate approach. This same resistance to harm means they can provide an unthreatened environment for students to practise in some of the more difficult areas of communication: areas such as giving bad news, coping with denial or anger, and dealing with embarrassment.

## Role playing

Within a stable group a lot of work can be done by role playing. Learners often lack experience of this method and even experienced doctors can be afraid of losing face, so that initial attempts may have to be taken sensitively but, once the first fears have been overcome, most people soon feel secure and find it an enjoyable and productive experience.

The very first stage for undergraduates may be to provide some very simple scenarios (a person with headache or a sore throat) and ask them to role play with a colleague within a very small group (possibly only one or two observers). In this way it is possible to look at greetings, question framing, and even simple negotiation of management.

Later, other uses of role play are possible. As well as more difficult management situations the group can be given scenarios which help them to look at aspects such as the breaking of bad news. These scenarios may be a patient returning for the result of a test, or a relative coming to the hospital not knowing that their father has died. With role play people have the opportunity to practise in a relatively safe environment

In these situations scenarios are provided by the tutors. Learners can also decide on roles they would like to portray. This is particularly helpful in giving them the chance to feel what it is like to be in the patient's shoes. Learners can be encouraged to choose a patient that they have seen with a difficult problem, then to role play that patient and report on what they felt about the 'doctor's' approach. In this way it is possible to learn, for instance, what it feels like for a heavy smoker to be bombarded by health education materials, or a 16-year-old girl who has a difficult relationship with her father to be faced with an older male doctor.

Allowing choice of situations enables the learners to adapt the learning to their own needs. In these circumstances it is wise to encourage them to put some distance between themselves and the role they take (i.e. undergraduates should not take the role of university students but rather of someone distanced by age, gender, or background). Role-play sessions are not the ideal place for people to try and resolve some of their own anxieties and worries about their health. At the same time it helps them to broaden their understanding of what other people may feel.

Once students are used to the concept of role play, it can be used as an adjunct to other teaching methods by asking students to briefly play a role in the middle of a group discussion.

## One-to-one reviews of consultations

Some units have facilities which allow one-to-one teaching on communication. Facilities for video-recording real interviews make it possible to go through consultations in fine detail. This is very time-consuming but can be very helpful, as long as certain guidelines are observed. Learner and teacher should be able to view the video in a relaxed situation, on the same level. It is often helpful if the student has control of the video control so that the student directs the learning, deciding when to stop and comment on an area. These areas may be either strengths or matters of concern. Above all, it is important that the positive feedback loop is observed.

Traditionally, consultations were judged by the records that were made. In enthusiasm for new approaches that help us to look in greater detail at the development of a relationship and at attitudes and skills, it is important not to neglect the written record. These can be used to explore a student's ability to summarize and present cases. We must remember that skills of recording, presenting, and dictating are important areas of communication for junior doctors.

## The timing of learning consultation

Formal teaching of communication was often introduced into medical schools by departments of mental health or general practice, even if these disciplines were taught late in the curriculum when students had received most of their experience in other disciplines. Of course, all disciplines have an influence on the development of expertise in communication, whether it be by informal input or simply by providing role models. Some disciplines have special interests, such as the paediatrician's concern with communicating with children and communicating through relatives. There is, therefore, a need to develop a pattern of teaching across the whole spectrum of clinical education, making use of the special opportunities provided by certain disciplines.

## The first contacts

Students need early and regular contact with patients if they are going to learn to see things from a patient's viewpoint. The first aim is to help them feel at ease talking to people from a variety of backgrounds who have health-related problems. When first arriving on wards, bedecked in white coats, students can feel inhibited if they feel that they lack the knowledge to talk to patients about medical issues. One way to overcome this is to encourage them (even from the time they enter medical school) to go and talk to sick people and ask questions at a very basic level. Long before they have to elicit a history of the presenting complaint or a detailed survey of the respiratory system, it is possible for them to ask a sick person the reason they have been admitted to hospital and how they feel about it.

When they reach the wards students can be very upset if one of the first patients they see is very ill, angry, or upset, so it is very important to make sure that patients chosen for these early contacts are willing and are not unduly tired. A patient who has already been seen by half a dozen health professionals in the day is unlikely to want to recount their story yet again to an anxious medical student. The student may get monosyllabic answers, and feel that clinical communication is difficult.

At the same time, students need to develop skills in the formal elicitation of information. Trying out different approaches in making relationships with patients, in question framing, and in ensuring that they do take a comprehensive history can be quite time-consuming. Until skills labs become more common in medical schools, much of the teaching will be in traditional situations, but encouraging students to use role play can be effective at the time they are first having to take histories. Selective use of simulated patients can help teachers to address the more difficult issues as they begin to arise. Finally, as students move towards finals, they should have the confidence to explore their communication through increasing use of video analysis, even on a one-to-one basis.

## After qualification

The need for reinforcing communication skills, and modifying them to deal with the new demands of medical work, has been constantly reiterated. It is important to give peer groups an opportunity to review these issues and relate them to the particular difficulties of a discipline (surgery, A&E, paediatrics, obstetrics, or geriatrics – all have different needs). Here the use of group task work, and particularly the use of role play, can be an ideal way if initial inhibitions can be overcome. Consideration may need to be given to ways to introduce other approaches such as video-recording. There are, however, considerable practical difficulties with this in hospital settings.

**Key points**

Communication will be learnt in many different ways. Students will learn from seeing other doctors at work. It is important to be aware of this 'modelling' and to make use of the opportunities to reinforce principles of good communication. A range of more focused approaches, from lectures to role play, can also be used. Student-centred feedback that builds on the strengths of individuals is central to these methods.

## Assessing results

Knowledge about communication can be assessed in traditional ways, but evaluation of attitudes and skills is more difficult. For too long the only means whereby the abilities of students to communicate effectively could be assessed has been by proxy approaches. These include the way that a student functions within a group, where it may be possible for tutors to assess attitudes and interpersonal skills to some extent, and the assessment of what they record and present about patient contacts. Whilst it is evident that being able to present a complete picture of the patient's problems does have some relationship to the ability to communicate, it may say as much about the patient's ability to give a succinct picture as about the student's skills. Some patients have told the story so often that they can rattle off a detailed history almost at the press of a button.

Watching a student talk to a patient can give some idea, but such a situation is unduly threatening and likely to be disruptive of the relaxed and normal atmosphere of communication.

The advent of video-recording (or audio tapes) has significantly altered the situation and enabled much more detailed assessments to take place. As with one-to-one teaching, students can make recordings of consultations with real or standardized patients. Review of these in detail can be used to assess their abilities in key areas.

A number of scales are now available for this purpose. One such scale looks at history taking, question style, structure of the consultation, listening skills, exploration of the patient's understanding and ideas and of their worries and concerns, explanation, checking that the patient understands, involving patients in decision making, and the overall relationship with the patient. Each parameter can be graded on a scale from unacceptable to very good.

The use of standardized patients can improve the reliability of such grading systems because each student is being tested under the same conditions. It is also possible for simulators to carry out the grading themselves or at least give some feedback on the performance of the student. This can be important for checking whether the student has the relevant patient-centred attitudes as a simulator can appreciate more effectively how a patient would respond to the approach taken by a particular student, also being able to compare the approaches of different students.

The main problem with such grading is the time involved. This is particularly true where a tutor has to evaluate a number of video recordings. When one-to-one video analysis is used as part of the learning experience feedback from even a single consultation has a value, but when the assessment is intended to be part of the final evaluation of the student, questions arise as to whether the sample of the student's skills which are viewed is large enough to give a reliable assessment.

There has, so far, been little work on the use of these methods to assess junior doctors but they are being introduced into professional assessments and examinations such as MRCP and MRCGP. The summative assessment of GP registrars at the end of vocational training now includes a consultation component where a number of real consultations have to be video-recorded and assessed using a scale. There is also a video-taped consultation component of the MRCGP examination.

## Summary

Developing interpersonal skills and attitudes is an awesome responsibility. If the consultation is the key moment of medical care, communication is the key to effective consultations. Perhaps our most effective input is to develop in students a level of self-awareness about the issues that will enable them to constantly review their view of patients and the approaches they use throughout their medical career. Students and young doctors will learn as much from the way we behave as from the formal teaching that we give. If the fundamental consideration in doctor–patient interaction is our view of the worth of patients and our desire to empower them, this will be demonstrated most clearly in our view of the worth of students and our desire to empower them.

### Key points

- Teaching communication should develop the learner's awareness of the need to adjust their views of patients and the approaches they use.
- Learners gain much from observation of the teacher's behaviour in communicating with patients and others.
- The aim of teaching communication is to enable the learner to provide effective, humane, and safe patient care.

- The strengths that the learner has should be used in developing communication skills.
- Learning communication means learning to respond in a patient-centred way.
- Learning communication requires self-awareness of strengths, weaknesses, and prejudices.
- Teaching communication begins with identification of the learner's own needs.
- 'Standardized patients' can be used to assess communication skills.

# 7 Assessment

## Tom Hayes

To many, educational assessment means the examinations they have had to face throughout their career. This chapter covers not only examination methods but also other forms of assessment, used at various points in an educational programme to either judge progress of the learner and the effectiveness of teaching or to determine whether the whole or part of training has been successfully completed.

There are many purposes for assessment:

- measuring improvements with time
- ranking, or giving a grade to students
- judging mastery of essential skills and knowledge
- identification of difficulties which students have with learning
- evaluating teaching methods
- evaluating the effectiveness of a course
- motivating students to study.

In addition, assessment is used to satisfy external bodies that the student has met required standards; and indirectly the general public.

Motivation of students to study has apparently been the main justification for frequent assessment of medical students; however, some of the methods used have often had a perverse and opposite effect to that intended by examiners. 'Assessment drives learning' is a regrettable truth; and many assessment methods drive students to rote learning and memorization of topics which it is guessed will be part of an examination. This criticism may also be levelled at the frequent use of multiple-choice questions (MCQs) in postgraduate examinations, which reinforce and perpetuate the habit of superficial learning at the expense of under-standing and problem-solving ability.

An ideal assessment would encourage undergraduates, those in postgraduate training, and the established practitioner to understand the topics under study, to appreciate how the new information fits into their existing knowledge, and how what is learned relates to present practice. These attributes will become increasingly important in assessing conti-nuing education and professional development for the purpose of reaccre-ditation.

# Definitions of assessment

## Formative assessment

The purpose of formative assessment is to provide information about the progress of the learner and the effectiveness of teaching. The need for further education is identified by the same process. Formative assessment is carried out during an educational or training programme with the intention of assisting learner and teacher, and should be perceived as neither judgemental nor threatening.

The outcome of formative assessment is primarily intended to help the learner and should, therefore, belong to him or her. The teacher may also be a joint owner of the assessment results if they are to be used for planning further training. The results of this form of assessment are not used to determine success or failure of the learner and are not, therefore, shared with any third party.

Formative assessment should be integral to the educational programme, providing feedback to the learner and teacher. These assessments should be carried out, formally or informally, at various points during the training programme. Their frequency will depend on the needs of the learner but should always occur towards the end of a module or block of education and training. Such terminal assessments should not, however, be perceived as an examination. Frequency will also be determined by the stage of training: those in basic training requiring assessment more frequently, possibly every three or four months, whilst those in the advanced stages might be assessed every six months or annually. Those in the phase of continuing education and professional development might find annual assessment helpful in planning their personal learning programme.

## Summative assessment

The purpose of summative assessment is determination of success or failure to complete a training programme. Such assessment provides valuable feedback to learner and teacher but this is not its prime purpose.

The results of summative assessment are needed by educational bodies responsible for setting standards of training programmes and the expected outcomes of training. Examinations set by these bodies rarely provide useful feedback to the individual learner. Indication of failure may be given in general terms: borderline or bad fail. This is usually of little help in advising the unsuccessful candidate on preparation for further attempts. Examiners fear that providing detailed information about reasons for failure may result in arguments about the examination process.

The concept that there is a continuum of types of assessment, ranging from those which are formative to those which are summative, is flawed. This changes the purpose of formative assessment, in particular if the outcome is used to decide whether the learner has achieved that standard expected by an outside body at a particular stage of training. It is important that there is not confusion between formative assessment, with its educational principles of feedback, and summative assessment, with its emphasis on success or failure.

## Validity

Instruments for assessment should be well founded; they should measure certain agreed items of knowledge, skills, or attitudes – and nothing else. To be considered valid an assessment method should be credible: measuring that which it is claimed it measures. Its content should also cover the range of subjects which it is intended to measure. The extent to which an assessment instrument measures various attributes is of importance in some examinations, particularly in discrimination between groups and as an indication of internal consistency.

Newer methods of assessment have to be tested against a suitable external measure to determine correlation. It is also valuable to determine whether there is a relationship between any method of assessment and the later outcome of education and training. Such predictive value of an instrument should not be confused with reproducibility of results, which determines the reliability placed on any assessment method.

Success or failure in an examination may be decided in one of two ways: whether the candidate meets a previously agreed standard, called criterion referenced assessment, or when it is decided that a certain proportion of those sitting the examination can pass, called norm referencing. Although the criterion referenced examination is clearly more fair, norm referencing is necessary to make decisions on awarding of prizes and when there is a limit to the number of candidates who can be allowed to pass and enter an advanced course, for example.

Whichever method for referencing is used, all who have an interest in the assessment procedure should be fully aware of how the candidate will be judged.

# Methods of assessment

## Formative assessment

Every student or other learner has a basic right to expect regular feedback on his or her performance but this is rarely put into practice. Ideally there should be an educational supervisor for each course or module of training, charged with the task of providing feedback based on formative assessments carried out by the supervisor or others. Teachers often, when challenged, reply that they do provide such feedback but surveys repeatedly show that this is not the view of those in training. This difference in perception probably arises because the trainers have not themselves received regular formative appraisal during their own training, feeling that what is required is a light-hearted chat whilst walking down the corridor or, with undergraduates, none at all. Those in training, however, recognize the need for personal, non-threatening feedback, focused on helping them to improve their performance.

Arguably the single most important advance in medical education, at least in the UK, would be to provide this feedback, in a structured manner. Effective feedback is likely to be achieved using the following ground rules:

- seeking the view of the trainee at the outset

- beginning with the positive or praiseworthy aspects

- dealing with specific problems rather than generalizations

- describing what has been observed and not what is inferred

- providing feedback as soon as possible after the observed activity or behaviour

- facilitating discussion of alternative tactics to help the learner to reach his or her own conclusions before providing advice, if necessary, on how best to correct deficiencies or poor performance

- providing protected time for both parties

- arranging the next review before the conclusion of the current process, including agreement on what has been achieved

- remembering that the interview is meant to be supportive and non-threatening whilst not avoiding difficult issues or problems which will be more difficult to deal with later.

*Rating scales* and *inventories* may be used as a means of formative assessment. These are of various kinds and are described, hereafter, in some detail.

The *global rating scale* is one of the most commonly used, particularly at the end of a module or term. Being of a general nature the scope is of little value for formative assessment unless made to address specific areas, expertise, or attitudes. If focused on a specific competency, such scales can provide valuable feedback, but such valid and reliable scales require considerable refinement and expertise. Rating scales devised for a particular group of trainees may not be applicable to others or to different circumstances until their validity and reliability have been confirmed in the other circumstances.

The *confidence rating scale* is used by the learner to indicate his confidence in his knowledge, skills, attitudes, or competence in relation to a specific topic. Such self-assessment/appraisal can form a valuable basis for a feedback session or in planning continuing education.

A third variety of scale is the *check-list*. This is essentially a restricted form of rating scale, but limited to two points in that the item has either been achieved or not. Check-lists are useful in monitoring progress through continuous assessment but are restricted in the amount of information that they provide. For example, they may indicate that the trainee has passed five central venous lines but give no indication how competent he is in performing this task. The logbook is a form of check-list. A suitable check-list can be agreed between the trainee and trainer at the beginning of an attachment or module, after both have agreed what experience should be gained and what learning should take place during the period.

*Self-completed rating scales* or *inventories* are useful if applied in a non-confrontational manner that allows the learner to answer truthfully. They are of particular value in self-assessment.

Rating scales have been frequently criticized. They do have advantages and disadvantages. In their favour is:

- they are economical to use and produce
- they can be validated and their reliability tested
- they may help introduce some standardization to teachers'/learners' assessment
- they can assess personal qualities which are not easily assessed by other methods
- they can be used for self-assessment by the learner
- they have been used for assessment, with success, in general practice.

Against the use of rating scales are:

- although reliability can be tested it is usually found that the inter-rates variability is high
- the ranges used, especially with global rating scales, are often too narrow and over 50% of those tested will often be rated above average
- they do not encourage raters to discriminate sufficiently between items on a multi-item scale; and there is a tendency for similar responses to all items rather than a discerning assessment for each individual item
- they may allow considerable observer bias
- they do not take account of differences in learning styles between the rater and the learner, nor different ways in which they process information.

For these reasons the effective use of rating scales requires special training in their use (and evidence that such training is effective).

Despite these criticisms, rating scales are likely to remain an important part of learner assessment. Their deficiencies must, however, be recognized. Design of rating scales is important if they are to be useful; and they are best used to evaluate those areas not easily tested by other means.

The conclusions from *clinical audit* may be a valuable means of assessing performance and as such may be a valuable educational resource. Most assessment processes measure knowledge or competence; they do not actually measure performance. Audit can, therefore, be a valuable means of assessment, with the proviso that it is understood there are many reasons why performance may be inadequate. There may be failure to translate competence into performance for organizational or attitudinal reasons, only some of which may be amenable to correction through education and training.

Whilst not an assessment procedure as such, *learning contracts* are a useful system for planning individual educational programmes, and can form the basis for subsequent formative assessment. These consist of a written document, agreed between learner and teacher, in which the latter specifies what the trainee will learn, how this will be accomplished, the timescale, and subsequent assessment.

The emphasis of the contract is upon agreement, both teacher and learner having an equal say in its content. For both parties to be able to do this they will need clear ideas on educational objectives of the training programme. Such contracts are not immutable, being subject to renegotiation by either party at any time.

Learning contracts have the advantage of flexibility, being designed to meet the needs of the learner whilst recognizing what is feasible in the learning environment. They give a sense of ownership to the learner, acting as a challenge and a stimulus to learning.

This written contract should form the basis for all formative assessment meetings between trainee and teacher. Within the contract there may be an agreement to use any or all of the other formative assessment tools.

A technique which is particularly appropriate for formative assessment, since it promotes active learning, is the *triple jump examination*. In the first part, the learner is asked to list the factors which need to be appreciated before a particular clinical, pathological, or similar situation can be understood. Having justified the choices, one is selected for further study. In the second phase, lasting days or weeks, the learner undertakes private study. Facilities are made available. In the final stage, the learner is presented with a series of short-answer questions related to the chosen topic. In answering the questions any notes or summaries which have been prepared during private study may be used, but not textbooks.

## Summative assessment

Some of the methods used for summative assessment may also be used for formative assessment, provided they are used to provide feedback, and to help in planning of further training.

*Oral examinations* have been used for assessment in medical education for many years but they have important defects. In the traditional viva the examiner has freedom to vary the questions between candidates and to decide what is the correct answer. Such assessments have poor reliability. Bedside clinical examinations are no better. Correlation between examiners is no better than would be expected by chance. For this reason the American National Board of Medical Examiners discontinued most such examinations.

*Vivas* do, however, allow for testing of certain skills. The viva examination needs to be fairly structured: questions asked should be agreed beforehand, standardized between candidates, and answers also agreed in advance. A series of short vivas, involving several examiners, marking candidates independently, is also a means of improving the examination and its fairness. The careful planning of oral and clinical examinations and substitution of objectivity and structure in place of the whims of the individual examiner will improve what is still regarded as a final rite of passage for undergraduate and postgraduate students.

Some examiners believe that the ability to present a cogent, literate response to a set question is an important attribute of an educated physician. Although not refuting the potential value of the *essay question*, it is well nigh impossible to produce evidence that this is a fair, valid, and reliable examination method. There is evidence of low correlation between rating between examiners; and thus the essay question has disappeared from most examinations.

If essay questions are used, it is important to prepare a detailed marking system, to be used by all examiners, usually in the form of a check-list. Setting essay questions also requires close attention, avoiding any ambiguity about what the examiner wants. Choice of questions, whilst favoured by candidates, poses the difficulty of ensuring that all questions are of equal difficulty.

*Multiple-choice questions* (MCQs) are widely used for the reason that they can rapidly assess a broad area of knowledge, and that they produce data which is easily analysed, often mechanically. If well designed they can have a high degree of reliability and validity; but it is difficult to write good MCQs and easy to produce bad ones.

The MCQs often only test discrete items of knowledge and not problem solving or understanding. Rarely do they test attitudes. They cannot test practical skills. They bear little resemblance to the work the successful candidate will be expected to perform. They also unfortunately promote rote learning. They test recognition of the correct answer(s) from usually five alternatives and not the recall of information which is required in practice. The MCQ does not test the uncertainties which abound in medicine, only accepting the correct answer. It is often said that success in a MCQ examination is more related to having learned the technique of answering such questions and not the knowledge base which the candidate has and which is supposedly being tested.

A critical former Professor of Medicine (Eichna) wrote about the use of MCQs in undergraduate examinations: 'They glorify facts, many of which are detailed, and some not necessary for a medical student but only for the expert in the field. Only menial thinking is needed. Problem solving is virtually absent.' Others speak as strongly of the value of the MCQ, claiming that it is adaptable to measurement not only of factual knowledge but also to problem solving, understanding, and judgement. It is rare to find such sophisticated examples of the MCQ.

Essay questions can be modified to improve reliability and validity. *Modified essay questions* (MEQs) were developed to avoid the cueing inherent in MCQs, where the candidate has to select from a number of alternatives. The stem question can be presented as a patient-management problem, thus giving relevance to the question. It is, however, difficult to write good MEQs which do not penalize the candidate throughout the remaining sections of the question for an incorrect answer at the beginning. Evidence is lacking for the value of MEQs in testing anything that cannot be done by MCQs, which are easier to mark.

Testing of the ability to solve clinical problems and diagnostic thinking, rather than mere recall of knowledge, is the reason for designing other methods such as *'grey cases'*, *data interpretation* questions, and *patient-management problems*. These methods are intended to overcome criticisms and deficiencies of other forms of assessment such as MCQs, MEQs, and essay questions.

The *objective structured clinical examination* (OSCE) is a very popular means of organizing an examination, and is not a method of assessment in itself. The OSCE can be organized to test practical clinical skills, problem solving, recall of knowledge, and communication skills. This format is now used in postgraduate as well as undergraduate examinations.

An OSCE consists of a series of stations with a test at each of these. Each station may contain a short MCQ, and require the candidate to demonstrate a particular clinical skill to the examiner, or to interpret an X-ray, ECG, or laboratory test. The examiner has a check-list for marking of candidates. Some stations may comprise the challenge of a simulated patient or a computer simulation. Other examination techniques apart from these may be used. Candidates move around the stations, in a given order, at pre-set intervals.

The OSCE has several advantages:

- it can be adapted to the needs of almost any specialty

- it standardizes assessment of skills

- its reliability and validity have been well evaluated.

There are some weaknesses of the OSCE arrangements:

- preparation requires great care and is time-consuming

- examiners must be trained, particularly in the use of check-lists, rather than their 'gut' reactions

- there is poor correlation with ratings of clinical performance, although good correlation with final marks when used in undergraduate examination

- there is uncertainty about the OSCE as a valid test of clinical skills.

*Video and audiotapes* can be used for both formative and summative assessments. Such tapes may be used in two ways: for the recording of performance and as an instrument in an examination.

Recording performance is valuable in allowing the results to be assessed, at leisure, by expert assessors. In addition, the tapes can be discussed with the learner. However, an audiotape is limited in its applications to testing history taking and communication skills but even then misses non-verbal clues. Some patients may be resistant to recording consultations and examinations; the written permission of patients should always be obtained.

When used as an examination tool, videotaped events can provide a standardized and economical instrument for examiners. It would, for example, be possible to include them in an OSCE. The evidence to support their use is, however, scant. Further work needs to be done on standardization of such methods if they are to be widely used for assessment. Videotapes are now being used as part of the final summative assessment of general medical practice trainees.

North American medical schools used *healthy people trained to simulate patients* very widely, both for examination and teaching purposes. There are now schools for training of those who act as simulated patients. Often referred to as standardized patients, they should not be confused with groups of real patients who have similar symptoms and signs and present the same challenge to candidates.

The standardized patient may carry out the assessment, or this may be done by independent observers. The rating given by a trained simulated patient may be a good test of interpersonal and communication skills. Such trained simulators are, however, expensive to hire.

*Computer simulations* are being developed in many specialties, particularly in the craft specialties. These have the advantage of providing a means for testing a variety of competencies in a standardized fashion. Although time-consuming to develop, once operational they could be economical. Sophisticated technology is becoming more available with the prospect of virtual reality. As computer simulation becomes more refined, it is likely it will play a greater role in both teaching and examination.

## Summary

In planning an assessment programme, whether it be for an individual to use as part of a self-assessment package or for formative assessment purposes amongst a group of trainees, whether at the end of a course or to satisfy the requirements of a licensing body, the wide range of methods should be remembered. All require careful planning.

The choice of technique must begin with an accurate definition of the purposes of assessment. Thereafter, the appropriateness and feasibility of the selected technique(s) should be considered. Finally, before any assessment instrument is used, it must be tested to ensure it is both a valid and reliable measure. In many ways, the quality of the assessment tool is of more importance than the method chosen.

**Key points**

- Any form of assessment requires careful planning.

- Choice of assessment method requires that the purpose is clearly defined.

- Formative assessment is intended to provide information about progress, the effectiveness of teaching, and the need for further education and training.

- Formative assessment is an integral part of education, providing feedback to teacher and trainee.

- Summative assessment is for the purpose of determining success or failure during a period or the whole of training.

- Summative and formative assessment are not part of a continuum.

- Validity of an assessment is an indication of its ability to assess what it is intended to assess.

- Regular feedback is a fundamental principle of good education.

- The conclusions of audit are a valuable measure of performance, and of value in assessing educational needs.

- A learning contract is a useful means of planning education.

- A learning contract is a valuable basis for formative assessment.

- The viva examination has poor reliability.

- A carefully structured viva permits examination of skills that cannot otherwise be assessed.

- MCQs test knowledge but not problem-solving skills or understanding.

# 8 Educational technology

## Tom Hayes and Joseph Campbell

## Introduction

The flood of new technology has produced a real danger of the technology seducing lecturers and teachers. We can then find ourselves trying to fit the education to suit the technology rather than the other way around. The correct approach is to decide your aims and objectives and consider the requirements of your potential audience. Only then should you choose a support technology, taking into account the facilities available to you.

High-tech methods may be high on interest but low in educational value. If your audience spends more time considering the marvels of the technology or wondering how you produced a particular effect rather than listening to educational messages, then the speaker's efforts and the audience's time have been wasted.

The following section deals with a number of different types of educational technology in outline.

## Slides and overhead projector transparencies

## General principles

The most common error is trying to put too much on the slide. Slides and overheads must be simple and to introduce a slide with an apology 'I know that there is too much on this slide but I want you to look at ...' is an insult to your audience; similarly with broken slides or damaged slides or those designed for a different purpose. It is better not to use slides at all if they are of poor quality. Some medical audiences consider a lecture without slides or overheads a pleasant change!

Simply photographing a graph or table from a book is not recommended, they very rarely make good slides since they were planned for a different medium. A difficult to understand slide or overhead project or transparency (OHP) is a distraction not a help.

## Slides

Many of the principles described in the following section dealing with OHPs and transparencies also apply to the use of 35 mm slides. Slides, although more expensive to produce and unable to be manipulated unlike that which can be achieved whilst using an OHP, have the advantage that they are more permanent, can be easily stored, and use colour more easily.

A useful guide for the amount of material in one slide is to limit text to no more than five lines. Tables should be reduced to the essential points; if you feel it is important that your audience has more detail this should be provided in handouts. Diagrams and illustrations should be clearly visible if the slide is viewed directly at arms' length. They should demonstrate the point you wish to make and non-essential material should be deleted.

Slides can be produced by different methods. Traditionally we have used either diazo slides, usually white on a blue background, and until recently colour slides for text were a luxury and were only used for illustrations or complex diagrams. The advent of computer-generated slides has altered all that. Most illustration departments report that the traditional methods of producing text or graphics slides are being rapidly overtaken by slides produced, usually by the lecturer, using computer graphics. The enormous possibilities for ornamentation and fancy graphics which this has produced carries with it its own dangers.

When producing slides using computer graphics, keep them simple and uncluttered. Avoid using a gimmick just because it is available. There is a real danger that you will produce slides where the audience is more interested in how you made them than the message you are trying to convey. If you are producing a series of slides try and use the same organization for all the slides.

Producing charts using computer graphics packages is easy – too easy. Slides using garish colours with multiscaled three-dimensional histograms are usually useless.

Making slides from computer discs requires expensive equipment in the illustration department. You can use instant slide-making techniques but these rarely produce the quality that is created by more expensive machines, the colours are usually less accurate, and the slides sometimes fade fairly quickly.

# Overhead projector transparencies

## Setting up and using an OHP

The major advantage of an OHP is that it allows the speaker to keep looking at his or her audience and avoids the necessity, which plagues the use of slides, of him turning his back to the audience. Yet how often do we see a person using an OHP as though it was a slide projector and turning away from the audience to look at the projected image on the screen? Therefore we have rule one for the use of OHPs.

## Producing transparencies

There are even more badly produced transparencies than there are appalling 35 mm slides! The faults are similar to those found with slides: too much material, text which is too small or otherwise illegible, figures which are too complex. They can all be avoided by a little thought. The principles which follow apply not only to the prepared transparency but also when a transparency is constructed during a presentation, perhaps to collect together the ideas from a group.

Just because a blank transparency seems large this does not mean that you fill it with large amounts of material. If you write the text yourself using felt pens, ensure that your writing is clear and the letters are about a quarter-inch tall, anything less than this will not be legible. Leave half to three-quarters of an inch between lines. Try using a grid to help you keep your writing straight; a sheet of graph paper beneath the transparency will help. If your writing is not clear ask someone with a good hand to copy your text. Water-soluble inks can easily be altered but are less permanent. To correct text or drawings done with spirit-based inks, use a medi-swab.

Transparencies can be produced by photocopying material from books or typescript on to special transparency film which is easily available. The risk here is to copy text which is too small or too densely packed. If you have to copy from a printed book, enlarge it first so that the text is at least a quarter inch tall and preferably taller.

Avoid the temptation to put too much on one sheet. Much better is to produce the text with a word processor using a suitable large font (at least 18 point and bigger for headings). Make sure that your printer is of good quality. Cheap dot-matrix printers give text which looks very cheap when enlarged on the screen.

It is possible to produce text for transparencies using rub-down letters such as Letraset, but unless you are an expert these tend to look a mess and can take a very long time to produce.

Transparencies are flimsy and can easily move around on the OHP or get squashed in your briefcase. For all but the most ephemeral of transparencies it is well worth putting them in a frame, indeed if you intend to write or draw on the transparency it helps to put the blank sheet in a cardboard frame before you start. The frame usually has notches cut in two edges which will allow you to align the transparency correctly on the pins which are found on the edge of most projector platens. Frames also have the advantage that you can write lecture notes on them.

Diagrams, tables, and figures for use with an OHP should be clear and uncomplicated. The lines used in drawings should be thicker than those used on the printed page, and so if you are copying from a book (remember the copyright laws) it may be necessary to thicken the outlines with a felt pen.

The staged revealing of the contents of a transparency using a sheet of paper on the OHP can be useful but infuriates some members of the audience.

## Videotapes

It is not possible here to go into great detail about the production of educational videos. Those that are produced commercially are the result of a great deal of production expertise and time spent by the content experts. It is not wise to try and emulate these videotapes unless you have such expertise and time at your disposal. That is not to say, however, that one should overlook the considerable educational opportunities which are available with a simple video camera when it is used imaginatively.

## Performance review tapes

Although we all expect video-tapes produced by someone else to be of the same quality as a BBC production, we and our colleagues do not expect the same standards from tapes which record our own activities. A simple VHS video camera is therefore of considerable value in such activities as monitoring our skills at interviews, clinical procedures, giving lectures, running tutorials, etc.

Such videos allow us, with agreement from the person(s) being recorded, to produce a video-tape which can then be played back for review by those involved. For instance, if a registrar continually fails to get a job because of poor performance at interviews then the recording of a mock interview can provide him with considerable insights into his problems and form the basis for useful discussions. Recording of a clinical procedure, whether it be inserting a pacing wire, carrying out a gastrectomy, or running an out-patient clinic, provides a similar opportunity. There are, however, certain ground rules for such activities:

- patients recorded in any video-tape should give their written permission

- the person whose performance is being recorded should be the first person to comment on the tape

- comments should be constructive rather than destructive

- unless specific permission is given the tapes should be erased after being used for the appraisal

- if the tapes are part of a teaching session for a group, all the members of the group should be video-taped and their tapes reviewed. It also is a good idea to include the tutor in such a group exercise and allow his performance to be appraised by the group.

## Tapes as triggers

Although many professionally produced video-tapes are designed to be seen through from beginning to end it is often possible to select from the tape sections which can be viewed, on their own, as trigger material for group discussions or to break up a lecture. Some tapes are produced specifically for this purpose. They are a potent stimulus to discussion.

## Interactive video discs

These discs hold vast amounts of data. They can contain up to 60 minutes of video or many thousands of still pictures plus sound. Linking this to a computer program to allow access to any part of the disc produces a potent teaching tool. However, the cost of producing such discs is enormous and they have yet to achieve a major breakthrough in postgraduate medical education.

## Conferencing techniques

These are techniques which allow groups at different venues to hear, view, and hopefully discuss the same material. The number involved in each site may vary depending upon the purpose of the conference from a single person to a full lecture theatre. The techniques used include, either singly or in combination, the following:

- audio conferencing
- video conferencing
- satellite television
- computer conferencing.

Whichever system is used, the crucial factor is that there must be interaction between those taking part – tutors and students. The audience must feel involved.

## Audio conferencing

This is the simplest and least expensive of all the systems. The various centres are linked together through the telephone system, using a 'bridge'. By the use of this 'bridge' each of the centres can hear what everyone else on the system is saying. The system can work anywhere in the world that is connected to a telephone.

Clearly, the use of speech alone has limitations but it is possible to run 'linked tutorials'. Each centre is supplied with visual material. Handouts, slides, or video clips work well, and the participants in each centre change the slides or use the video clips as instructed by the tutor.

Interaction is easy as long as no more than about ten centres are involved. Questions can be put by the tutor to each centre in turn or comments can be requested, but the tutor must ensure that all the centres are involved. This involvement is essential so that the barriers raised by the technology are overcome.

## Video conferencing

Clearly this has advantages over audio conferencing but it has the major disadvantage of a higher cost, although systems linked to ordinary computers are improving rapidly. Most of the commercial systems currently in place use dedicated lines with a high data transmission capacity and involve a limited number of fixed sites. However, the widespread use of video conferencing for educational purposes may not be far away.

## Satellite television

Satellite television on its own does not provide conferencing facilities except for centres equipped with both satellite downlinks (the common or garden satellite dish, albeit usually rather larger than the domestic variety) and an uplink which will transmit pictures up to the satellite. Although mobile uplinks are in use by major television companies and by some educational centres in the United States, they are not in day-to-day use by centres in this country. The compromise of satellite television with audio links between the production centre and the receiving centre is, however, in common use with such systems as EuroTransMed.

Whilst the production costs of ventures such as this are beyond most peoples' resources, the recently developed concept of narrowcasting (in contrast to broadcasting) may have a place in the future. It is now possible for satellites to restrict their transmission to fairly small areas and this means that transmission could be sent to groups who would all know those involved. This will make the presentation more acceptable, in the same way that we view our home videos in quite a different way to our expectations from a *Horizon* programme. With the costs of sending programmes via satellites coming down all the time it is conceivable that a region or group of regions could put together programmes which meet local needs at a reasonable cost. Interaction will remain critical, even if it is via audio links, otherwise you might as well distribute video tapes.

## Computer conferencing

The use of real-time computer conferencing is becoming more popular and the use of bulletin boards is increasing, and they may have educational uses.

## The Internet

The Internet and, in particular, the World Wide Web are now becoming ubiquitous and the educational potential is considerable. However, apart from searching for information through databases such as Medline or BIDS, the other opportunities are used by a minority. The number of continuing medical education (CME) programs and other educational material has risen substantially in the last few years and seems destined to grow further.

The ways of using these resources are developed further in the next section.

# Computer-aided learning

The rate of technological advance and the changing nature of clinical practice continues to alter the training needs of health professionals. There is continuous pressure to assimilate a knowledge base that seems to increase exponentially. Computer-aided learning (CAL) offers a variety of ways to meet these changing needs and a means to access, organize, and analyse the growing body of health and medical knowledge.

CAL has many applications, ranging from the direct delivery of instruction, to helping teachers cope with their role, to a tool to directly support the learner. Each of these is dealt with in the sections that follow. However, the price of personal computers and software remains fairly high, and the time necessary to learn how to use both hardware and software means one must decide carefully where to invest time and money in CAL.

# Computers as teaching tools

Computers have some characteristics that make them eminently suitable for teaching. They allow the learner to work at his or her own pace, they can provide immediate and detailed feedback, and they don't humiliate. This potential, however, is only realized when appropriate educational theory is applied to content that matches curricular needs. This must all be presented as an error-free program that has an intuitive, interactive, user-friendly interface.

It is clear that the characteristics of good educational software demand more than the skills of most amateur software designers. Even with special software designed to facilitate the production of educational materials, it can take a team of educators, clinicians, and programers 300 hours to produce just one hour of computer-based teaching material.

The problem with prepackaged software, however, is that there is a steep correlation between quality and price, and most software is difficult to customize. Despite such restrictions there are still some worthwhile packages to consider. Drill-and-practice packages can be a very cost-effective and practical way to improve and test basic scientific knowledge of academic subjects such as anatomy or biology. There are, for example, sophisticated multimedia programs that allow learners to explore anatomy in ways that would be impractical or impossible in other ways. The Open University is producing an interactive multimedia tutorial on the brain and nervous system on CD-ROM, for use in its Biology: Brain and Behaviour course. It contains short video clips with pro-sections and video rotations of anatomical features that can be controlled by the learner. It will also have a built-in self-test that generates multiple-choice questions (MCQs) on the CD-ROM's contents.

Another particularly useful and effective type of CAL program is the simulation. Computer simulations enable learners to interact safely with complex or dangerous systems, for example running simulated heart attacks and applying different treatments. The University of Wollongong, Australia has, for example, produced a chemistry laboratory simulation, called OzChem, that prepares students for laboratory exercises and is a prerequisite to laboratory entry. Given the high prices of chemicals and the difficulties of using animals in experiments, laboratory and medical experimental simulations are a viable alternative to traditional approaches to bench work.

A good source for learning more about these and other types of software is the Computer Teaching Initiative's (CTI) Centre for Medicine. Its address is University of Bristol, Royal Fort Annexe, Tyndall Avenue, Bristol BS8 1UJ. It can be reached by e-mail on CTICM@bristol.ac.uk.

## The computer as a tool to aid the teacher

CAL also encompasses the use of the computer as a teaching and management aid. One advantage of a computer over other media is that it allows data to be stored and easily manipulated. Student records are one area where computer packages such as databases can be particularly time-saving. Most databases can be designed so that any given piece of data, for example a name or an assessment grade, need be entered only once. Thus a mark for an assignment, after it has been recorded once, can appear automatically in report forms, exam-board summaries and letters to students. This is a feature which is of particular value to teachers who have students attached to them for short periods but who need to keep a record of their performance. Popular, affordable databases offering good value for money include Microsoft Access and Filemaker Pro by Claris Corporation.

The use of computers to produce handouts, overhead transparencies, and slides is covered in earlier sections of this chapter.

## The computer as a learning-support tool

The final area of CAL to mention is the computer as a learning-support tool. The computer is no longer just a data processor. It is also a communication tool. It is standard for many computers to be linked to larger computer networks with software that supports access to information resources such as the Internet and to other people via e-mail. Both the Internet and e-mail are relatively new technologies, and their potential to enhance medical education is enormous.

E-mail offers new opportunities for tutorial and peer support that can be realized through personal communications or e-mail-based discussion groups. The Internet offers access to large databases of medically relevant information such as the Cochrane database, Medline, and the *British Medical Journal* to name a few. The problem is that finding good information often takes time. This, however, is being overcome by initiatives to systematically review the quality of information that is provided. A far greater challenge to the availability of such information, however, seems to be finding effective methods to employ it to improve learning. Having access to more information will not help learners unless that information is relevant to their learning needs. This is as true with these new technologies as it is with the computer as teaching tool and teacher-support tool.

## Multimedia techniques

These allow the computer to produce sound and video presentations either alone or by linkage with other equipment. The systems are not yet standardized but rapid strides are being made and it seems likely that these will become a potent educational tool, especially for learning by the individual. The production of multimedia packages is likely to remain the field of the expert for some time.

## Virtual reality

This technique, which is beginning to be used more widely, especially for games, is very likely to play a major role in teaching skills in the future. Experiments are already underway in the use of virtual reality in teaching surgical procedures.

Linking virtual reality with conferencing brings about what is being called 'telepresence'. The potential for such a technique makes the mind boggle.

# Educational facilities

## Lecture rooms/theatres

The ideal lecture theatre would have the following features:

- a shape that would allow all those present to view the screen easily; this may require the theatre floor to be raked but this will limit the use of the theatre for other events. The section on screens later in this chapter contains further information

- acoustics that would allow the audience to hear the speaker. If amplification of the lecturer's voice is needed this should be foolproof. The microphone should either be sensitive and multidirectional or an inconspicuous clip-on microphone which does not destroy the speaker's clothes. Microphones which attach the speaker to the lectern by a lead are undesirable as active lecturers have been know to destroy the equipment or injure themselves by moving around more vigorously than the lead will allow

- a lectern that combines the facility to hold the lecturer's notes and the switches for the audio-visual equipment but does not provide a barrier behind which a nervous speaker can hide from the audience. The design of lecterns is an art which most venues have not acquired. Many require the speaker to have a prolonged course of instruction before they can use the switches for the lights, projectors, etc. efficiently

- a well-placed OHP. The placing of the OHP requires some thought. It is often placed so that either the lecturer cannot get to it or if he or she uses it incorrectly the audience cannot see the screen! If you need to tilt the screen for the correct use of the OHP (see later in this chapter) but not for the 35 mm slides then consider using a separate screen

- blackout facilities and the ability for the speaker to adjust the level of lighting. Although it is desirable always to have some light so that the lecturer can see the audience and because total darkness is very soporific, there may be occasions when the speaker needs total darkness to show a particular slide such as a pale histology sample. Speakers should be aware of the risks of prolonged total darkness.

The following equipment should be available for use in all lecture theatres:

- slide projector
- overhead projector
- screen
- pointer
- blackboard or whiteboard
- video recorders, both VHS and Umatic, plus enough monitors or a video-projection system.

Some of the items above are dealt with in the next section.

# Slide projectors

The most common slide projector in use in postgraduate centres is undoubtedly the Kodak carousel in one of its many guises. It can be bought with a variety of lenses, with attachments for remote control via an infrared link, with links for automatic operation, dual projection, etc. It comes in various weights depending upon how much metal is in the case. The best advice is to buy the strongest and least complicated version you are likely to need. An infrared link avoids the problems of lengths of wire connecting the speaker with the machine.

## Lenses

If you are likely to use the projector in more than one venue, buy a zoom lens which will allow you to adjust the image to fill the screen. If the projector is fixed in the lecture theatre, buy a lens of appropriate focal length so that the image is of the maximum possible size for the screen. The bigger the lecture theatre the longer the focal length needed.

# Overhead projectors

These are among the most used and the most abused of audio-visual aids found at medical meetings.

## Selecting an overhead projector

These are basically simple pieces of equipment but often they are required to stand up to a great deal of use. In selecting one, make sure that spare bulbs are easily available, that you can replace the bulb easily, and that the adjustment to focus the bulb is accessible. Some machines carry a spare bulb which can be brought into play by a switch if the other blows. Most machines have a wattage of around 250 but if you intend to use a computer-driven LCD screen (see below), or have a large lecture theatre, 400 watt machines are available.

Transportable machines which save weight and bulk by having the light source in the head are useful if you have to move the OHP between different buildings.

Try and listen to a machine in action if you are considering buying since a noisy fan which goes on for a long time after the projector is switched off is the bane of both lecturer and audience alike.

### Setting up an overhead projector

A problem seen all too often with OHPs is the distorted image. This is usually when the top of the image is wider than the bottom and is due to the OHP being too low as compared to the screen. Depending upon the nature of the room being used it may not be possible to raise the projector, then the best solution is to tip the top of the screen forward.

Another form of distortion is when colour fringes appear on the screen and this can be adjusted by refocusing the lamp. In modern OHPs this can usually be done using a knob on the outside of the machine, but in older or cheaper projectors it may be necessary to open them to make this adjustment. Beware of a hot bulb and live wires when you do this!

## Computer-driven LCD projectors and screens

These are excellent for demonstrating computer programs and can be used with computer graphics packages to present 'slide shows'. This allows the use of fancy fade techniques between slides and for the projected image to have sophistication.

They are expensive but though the quality of the image that the best projectors now produce is quite reasonable they are not as good as a conventional slide projector. However, the ability to change rapidly the order of slides, use fade and build techniques, and highlight areas under discussion means that these projectors are becoming increasingly popular.

The stand-alone projectors give a brighter image than those used with an overhead projector and can also show video-tapes. If a liquid crystal display (LCD) screen is used with an overhead projector then a higher power projector (usually 400 watt) is necessary.

## Screens

There are a number of different types of screen: matte, ultra matte, lenticular, beaded, etc. The brightest image is given by the lenticular screens but they are directional and therefore this limits their use somewhat. Many experts now believe that a flat wall painted with brilliant white paint is an excellent substitute, and if the area painted is wide enough it can cope with dual projection.

The size of the screen should be large enough so that no one has to sit nearer than twice its width or further away than six times its width.

## Pointers

Whilst the billiard cue or extending ball-point pens given away by drug companies will work satisfactorily in small rooms, for a lecture theatre a light pointer is needed. The best of these today is a laser pen. One problem is that the battery operated versions not only need to have their batteries changed but they have a tendency to be 'lost'. Mains-driven pointers stay in the lecture theatre but do tie the lecturer to the lectern.

## Other facilities

Do not forget the blackboard, often white or green these days. If you use a whiteboard do not write on it with spirit-based markers. If you use chalk and a blackboard, make sure you have a duster handy.

---

**Key points**

- High-tech methods may be high in interest but low in educational value.

- Avoid the temptation to put too much information on a transparency.

- Video-tape may be used to review performance and to trigger group discussion.

- Conferencing techniques are only successful if the audience is involved.

- Multimedia computer programs can be helpful in teaching anatomy.

---

# Glossary

| | |
|---|---|
| **Cognitive** | explaining learning in terms of knowing and under-standing, as opposed to attitudes or skills |
| **Competence** | ability to do a task; but not necessarily how the task is done/performed |
| **Domain** | scope or field of learning – knowledge, skills, and attitude |
| **Facilitation** | helps learning and understanding |
| **Heuristic** | encouragement to learn through personal discovery |
| **Jesuitical** | learning through inference and influence |
| **Performance** | carrying out of task(s), unrelated to ability |
| **Precept** | command, principle, rule of conduct, or truth usually based on experience |
| **Socratic** | learning through question and answer; encouraging the learner to display knowledge in response to questions |
| **Validity** | soundly based, e.g. assessment |

# Index